UNLEASHED

A STORY ABOUT A WOMAN LEAVING BEHIND SOCIETY'S STANDARDS AND RECONNECTING TO HER OWN DRUMBEAT

CLAUDIA STÖCKLER

Copyright © 2023 by Claudia Stöckler

All rights reserved.

All rights reserved. Apart from any fair dealing for the purposes of research or private study, or criticism or review as permitted under the Copyright, Designs, and Patents Act 1988, this publication may only be reproduced, stored, or transmitted, in any form or means, with the prior permission in writing of the copyright owner, or in the case of the reprographic reproduction in accordance with the terms of licenses issued by Copyright Licensing Agency. Enquiries concerning reproduction outside those terms should be sent to the publisher.

ISBN # 978-1-7371719-8-0

CONTENTS

Introduction	v
1. Being caught in between	1
2. My drumbeat is different	9
3. Breaking free: Strike 1	19
Summer, Sun, Barcelona	
4. When society's "good life" doesn't fit	27
5. Breaking free: Strike 2	35
Rekindling my feminine side	
6. It is ok to fall and ask for help	47
7. Breaking free: Strike 3	55
Alternative community living gone wrong	
8. A deeper initiation	63
9. The meltdown realization	71
10. Trust and magic will happen	81
11. Life is too short not to live according to your terms	89
Acknowledgments	93
Thank you	95
About the Author	97

INTRODUCTION

Hello, courageous Soul!

I am so happy that you are reading this book!

I am writing from this gorgeous campsite in North Queensland, Australia, where I just arrived. It is surrounded by one of the world's oldest rainforests and is truly beautiful. I feel so blessed sitting here on lush green grass between palm trees and paperbark trees, looking out on a little lake. At the moment, I am the happiest and most content version of myself, which I haven't been in a long time. I feel like everything is falling into place for me at the right time, and if it is not falling into place, it is not the right moment yet. But I know it is coming, and I have non-shattering trust in that.

My living space is my little car, a 2001 Subaru Forester. It is a small space, but it has everything I need. I have a built-in bed with drawers and storage that a very kind Australian carpenter I met one day on another campground offered to build for me. I have with me some clothes, a chair, a yoga mat, some cooking utensils, personal care items and other personal stuff. That's all I

INTRODUCTION

really need. I have been traveling and living in my car, which I lovingly call "Susi, the Subaru," for two and a half months now, and I love it. It is the smallest living space I have ever had, but it gives me so much freedom, which is what I love about it. I value freedom over anything. I love that I can pack up my things, go anywhere, and stay as long as I want. Apart from that, I am a true nature lover. I love being outside all day, every day. I feel so much more alive and connected in my being. I wake up and start each day slowly, enjoying a nourishing breakfast along with a cup of coffee or cocoa. I cherish the first hour of the day, spending it in nature. I love that I no longer have to rush to be somewhere at a certain time in the morning. This was a part of my life for many years, and I never liked it. It felt confining. So I really cherish mornings like these. They have become such a sacred time to me that I try to protect them. How I start my morning sets the tone for the rest of the day. I know this sounds amazing, and most days, it truly is like that, and I feel super grateful and blessed.

With everything, though, there is another side to it. Not everything is rainbows and sunshine all the time. I want to be honest with you and not paint a romanticized, perfect Instagram picture of living on the road. There are days when it just sucks, especially when I am in an area where it has been raining for days; everything is humid and wet, and I don't really have a place to hang out except for the two front seats of my car. Or when I am in an area that gets really cold and I have to put on layers and layers of clothes, a beanie and crawl into my bed at 6 pm with a warm water bottle to protect myself from the cold. The days that it sucks the most are during my menstruation when I just want to have my own space to withdraw, have access to a clean bathroom and shower all to myself, not having to share with strangers or animals like mosquitos, spiders, snakes or frogs. But that's life, I suppose; blissful days and shitty days coexist,

INTRODUCTION

whether you are camping in nature or if you live in an apartment. There is an unbeatable feeling of freedom, and I would not change how I live for anything else in the world. I am free to do whatever I want whenever I want. There are no unspoken expectations I have to fulfill to fit into the picture of being a good citizen. Everything is my choice! I am the creator of my life. This is one of those phrases I have heard repeatedly and only understood mentally, but never truly in my body until now. Now, I truly embody it, and I am super grateful and feel very blessed for that. As I write these lines, I can feel life and vibrancy in my whole body coming online. It even makes me tear up a bit because I am so damn grateful and happy that I have endured all the bullshit that, to be fair, I partly chose for myself, but I did it anyway.

I did it anyway!

That is key!

And now I am here!

Truly living and embodying it.

And you can too!

The question is, do you dare to?

I say you do! Otherwise, you wouldn't be holding this book in your hands. Even though you might not entirely feel it yet, I am telling you that by reading this book in right now, you've already taken the important first step. You know that you want to change something in your life, but you don't know how yet. Well, guess what? That is absolutely ok! You don't need to have all the answers right away. The fact that you've purchased this book marks a significant first step. Take a moment to celebrate that accomplishment! Celebrate yourself for taking action and initiating this process. Giving ourselves more recognition and

INTRODUCTION

celebration in life is crucial, even for the seemingly small steps we take. By purchasing this book, you have embarked on a vital journey toward your personal freedom and aliveness. Get ready to be inspired!

Even though travel is a major part of my life, this is not your average travel book for tips and tricks or what to do in different countries. There are other beautiful books for that. This is my story about feeling lost and stuck in a world that I didn't really fit into and my many attempts to break free and feel the most alive I have felt in a long time. This is my story of challenges and hardships and learning what I want in life, what I deserve, and what I'm worth. It is the story of how I am finding myself again by leaving behind what society says I should want and figuring out what I actually desire in this life. It is a story of me falling on my face many times, falling back into old patterns, shaming myself about that, but also always being guided by the universe and my own drumbeat of freedom, guiding me back to my true aliveness.

My deepest wish is that you feel seen and heard in your own life and that you are not alone in this. I also deeply hope to inspire you to take action toward owning your best life.

This is my love letter to you.

This is hopefully inspiration for you to live an extraordinary and magical life.

This is your permission to follow your heart, even though it might sometimes seem impossible and you don't know where to start.

This is your sign to finally leave that "good life" that society has told us to be happy with, break free, and live on your terms.

This is your sign to carve out your own path.

INTRODUCTION

This is your sign to break free of the "good girl" mask and go live wild, free and magically in whatever form will be the best for you!

This is your loving reminder that the life of your dreams is on the other side of your fear.

I faced a lot of fears within myself, but also from others.

I faced a lot of doubts within myself, but also from others.

I faced many limiting beliefs and still do today, but I no longer allow myself to be held back by them.

I faced so many people who told me what I can and cannot do in life.

I faced so many people who wanted me to stay small and not shine my light.

I faced family members insulting, screaming and shouting at me, telling me I was stupid, naive and didn't have my shit together.

I faced so many who wanted to force their way of living onto me without considering what I wanted and needed.

I faced so much rejection and backlash, especially from close loved ones.

I faced many who told me my way of living was wrong because I broke out.

I triggered their pain.

I triggered their fear.

I triggered stuff that they didn't want to look at. That's why they freaked out and wanted me to stay small, accommodate and continue to please everyone else, and be without my own needs. They wanted me to stay in my assigned "good girl" role,

INTRODUCTION

to be easily manipulated and pushed around according to their needs.

So I broke free, left and traveled to different countries and learned a lot about other cultures and how people live their lives in different ways, and it fascinates me to this day. Being outside my usual environment also gave me the necessary distance, time and space to get to know myself better and figure out what I want. The patterns I adopted growing up in my family and the society are running deep through me and were dictating my life until I really started to look at them. After all, I am 34 years old at this moment, which means the patterns had about three decades of playing out. I cannot change them overnight or over a couple of years, and that is absolutely ok. We're all humans, we make mistakes and sometimes we just need a little longer to understand certain things. I fell back into my patterns of self-doubt over and over again. In fact, over the course of a few years, it took me four rounds of falling back into old patterns and creating immense amounts of suffering for myself before it clicked that I could stand up for myself and what I want in life. This drumbeat of aliveness, vibrancy and freedom has been an essential thread guiding me every step of the way. Even when I have tried to quiet it, avoid it, ignore it, push it down, it was always there lingering in the background, not leaving me alone and becoming louder and stronger every time I tried to push it away.

To this day, some family members are still trying to tell me how I need to live my life. A good job and an apartment represent security and stability to them, and I understand why they would want that for me, but I want more in life! I want to feel alive, vibrant, fulfilled, nourished and free. Not stuck in a soul-sucking 9-5 job, living in an overly expensive apartment, only working to afford things that we have been told would make us happy, but trap us. I tried that and it slowly took away my life force, drop

INTRODUCTION

by drop. From a very early age, I told myself I wanted to live a magical and fun life. On my deathbed, I want to be smiling and saying, "What a hell of a ride," not having any regrets of missing out on something or wishing that I had done more of other things.

Everything in this book is based on my challenges, hardships, learnings and experiences. I am a woman who wants to speak from my own embodied truth and experience.

So lean back and enjoy the ride. :)

PS: Dancing and music are a big part of my life and have helped me through many ups and downs. I love connecting with people through music, so I decided to put a song at the end of every chapter that encapsulates the emotions or the essence of that chapter. I would like to invite you to find and listen to that song after reading each chapter.

Right now, I invite you to listen to:

"In this together" - Emily Roberts, STENGAARD, Pyke & Muñoz

At the end of the book I have provided a way to access the playlist

I dedicate this book to all the courageous souls holding it in their hands. Who wants to follow their own drumbeat and create a beautiful, magical and vibrant life according to their own terms.

ONE
BEING CAUGHT IN BETWEEN

I AM 34 years old right now, and I don't know about you, but I often find it difficult to navigate life and find my own way. I am walking on a path that no one in my family has walked before. I very often feel lost and have no idea what I am doing. I feel a lot of shame around that because I should have figured life out by now, like my parents did when they were my age. But it was a different time back then, and it was much more common to go the "usual" society paved way of creating a home by the time they were 30 years old. Even when I compare myself to friends of the same age who have created a family and home by now, I sometimes feel like they have "life figured out." Then again, what does that phrase even mean? According to society's standards, they have life figured out, and I definitely don't. I am in my mid-30's, living in my car — the smallest space I have ever owned — going from camp spot to camp spot in nature, exploring Australia, and only owning just the most basic things. This is not exactly how my family or society told me to live my life. But I haven't felt so happy, content and truly free in a long time. So, according to society's standards, I haven't figured it out at all, but according to my standards, I don't need to. How I see it, "having life figured out" is not a destination but an ongoing day-to-day process of continuous learning. I am constantly figuring out how I want my life to be and how I want to live it.

Yet sometimes, old patterns sneak back in and tell me that this is not good enough. I have created new lives with friends, communities, and experiences in six countries on two continents; this is my seventh country on my third continent now. I am meeting amazing people, creating beautiful new friendships, having wonderful experiences, constantly learning about myself, and expanding my horizons. I love that. This is what I am truly passionate about. It ignites my fire, creativity, aliveness and vibrancy. Still, it is not easy to constantly live like that. Many of the changes happening in my life can be unsettling— bringing discomfort and many goodbyes. Yes, I know "The only constant in life is change" or "You have to create stability within yourself first." I have heard those phrases so much that I can't hear them anymore. Yes, they are true to a certain extent, but if you are truly living the lifestyle that I am, and you are faced with change all the time, there are usually moments when you feel lost. I ask myself, "What is wrong with me? Why can't I be happy with a house, a spouse, kids, a stable job, and just some comfort?" Truth be told, I can't! Unfortunately, I just can't see myself fitting into society's way of living life and being happy. And believe me, I have tried!

Actually, I tried four times and it certainly did not make me happy. I actually felt miserable as if life was being extracted from me. But somehow, there is still a little voice inside of me telling me that the way I am doing things is wrong. The shift I see is being more conscious about our health, not only physically but also mentally. Becoming more conscious about how we spend our time creates more balance in our work and life. I feel generations after mine don't want to spend 40-60 hours in an office working for someone else anymore; it feels life-extracting to them, and I totally get that. I don't want that either for myself. Life is not only for work, especially in my most precious years and for someone else's company and dream. I want more!

But here I am sitting, internally struggling between the traditional values passed down to me from my previous generations but also yearning for something more. I feel like we, in our late 20s to our early mid-40s, grew up with parents still embodying those values of working hard, going to church, being a good citizen and obeying the rules of the government and the church. They defined themselves through their work and accomplishments, first and foremost. I see it in my parents, aunts and uncles, and teachers. I saw it a lot in the company I worked for in Switzerland, where people committed to this one job for decades. That's what they learned from their parents who learned it from theirs, and so on. Those are hundreds and thousands of years of old patterns that won't change overnight or over a couple of generations. It will take many generations to change the old way of living. I see that the change is coming, but slowly. I have to remind myself that it has only started and it is ok not to want the old, even though I don't yet know what is next.

An important point to mention here is shame. I feel that there is still a lot of shame being created around not wanting to commit for decades to the same job in the same company, especially from older generations. At least, that is what I saw in my family and in the village I grew up in. I remember one day, after hiking with my father, we went into a typical Austrian alpine hut in the mountains in summer, and a woman from our village came to sit with us for a little chat. The woman was working at the local bank, and complaining about how the younger generations don't want to work anymore. She said young people don't know what hard work is anymore and they did not want to put in the hours.

I was just sitting there, watching and listening, not saying anything, and just thinking to myself, "I would not want to do that either." I'm not saying anything against working hard or that I am not willing to put in the hours, but it needs to be for something that feels fulfilling, with purpose, igniting my heart. For me, that is a whole different story from just working for some company eight to ten hours a day. Apart from that, I also want to enjoy my life now when I am young and fresh instead of waiting for retirement to do what I want. Life is happening now, and I want to make the most out of it. I sensed a lot of frustration in this woman while she was sharing. I can only assume that she was shaming the younger generations for not being like her as a protection mechanism because she does not allow herself the same kind of things, but deep down, she might want it too. We all carry shame, in and around different issues, and it is very often the shame we feel that holds us back in life. Also, being shamed by others for not being like them or like society wants us to be can create a lot of internal shame and anxiety, potentially holding us back from living the life we want.

We are in a paradigm shift where people don't want to do this anymore because they want more, and so do I. Going to school, studying and then committing to this one job and staying there for my entire life to afford the home, cars, holidays and anything else we feel we need to be happy can't be it. That can't be all there is to life! And I am not blaming or shaming. That's what we have been told to do for generations. But I want to spend my life experiencing the beauty of it. I want to have adventures when I am young. I want to follow my passion and deep, innate desires in all aspects of life. I want to wake up in the morning and be excited about what I will create. I want to go to bed at night and feel fulfilled in what I have done. I want to be an inspiration to those coming after me. I feel like the more I walk down this path, the more I connect with my purpose of serving others to inspire and invite them to follow what sets their hearts on fire. I always had the feeling there was more out there, but the thing is, since I also grew up with those traditional values, I only have an inner knowing/feeling that there is more out there, but I don't know where or how to find it. That is the difficult part for me and so many others in my generation. Unfortunately, there is no "How to find something more in life" manual, I have searched for it. If you have it, please share it with me! We are creating our own path with the inner struggle of the old and the new. A struggle that younger generations don't have as much, in my opinion.

Like I said, I am in my mid-30s right now, and I have to say I relied on my parents more than I am comfortable admitting. Honestly, I also feel a bit ashamed of sharing it here for everyone to read, activating my fear of being judged and canceled. I always prided myself on being independent from a young age. I became hyper-independent and put up a lot of walls. But to be radically honest with myself and you, I had the privilege of doing that because my family had my back. I always had a place to return to, an empty apartment to live in, a safety net in the background, and I relied on it. The last time was just before I came to Australia. I was staying in an empty apartment, for which I did not pay rent, which helped me save up for this upcoming trip to Australia. There were other times in the past as well. I took these opportunities for granted but was never really grateful for them. Not because I am or was an ungrateful person, but instead I didn't fully acknowledge and accept the fact that I had this beautiful opportunity. I tried to conceal and paint it in a different light because I was ashamed of being a woman in her late 20s, and beginning 30s, still relying on her parents. I felt ashamed because where I grew up, I was shamed for this from an early age. I was treated like an outsider for most of my early years because my parents earned pretty well, and it came with a lot of privilege for me and my brother. It makes me feel a bit immature and not adult enough. It is also not something I am very eager to admit in this book, but I am doing it anyway because I am committed to being honest and vulnerable here.

I also can say that even though I chose not to go down this path of committing to a house, a stable job and the preached stability that society tells us we need, I am eternally grateful for my family always having my back, being my safety net and always giving me a place to return.

Instead of going society's way, I chose to go on many escapades to find my "something more to life." I found it in many different cultures and countries, but it somehow was never "good enough." I was eagerly searching for the best version of life, motivated by the lack I felt in Austria. I was also falsely motivated by the romanticized picture of always being happy and fulfilled, so I searched for the best way to have that. Only now have I come to realize that it doesn't exist…who would have known? It is in my own hands to find out what values I want to live by and what kind of person I want to be. I am still figuring that out, and I love it because I have accepted that it is a constant process of growing and glowing. A friend of mine told me once, "You are such a complex person. It is never going to be linear with you." At first, I was a bit shocked by that, but then I looked back at my life and it was true. It hasn't been a linear line so far; now that I have accepted that, I can see the beauty in it. Actually, I love that it hasn't been and probably never will be a linear path for me, and I love that I don't know what will happen next. It makes my life more exciting and open to invite more magic.

In the four times I went back to try to live in Austria, I struggled and mainly blamed my surroundings for not being what I needed them to be. While it is important to acknowledge that some surroundings are just not right for my own growth, it is no one's fault but rather a compatibility issue. It is equally important to look at myself, be honest, and see my role in this as well. There is no shame in it. It just simply is. I had this inner struggle with the old and traditional values that I had learned as a child and the almost desperate wanting of "something more" but, at the same time, not really taking action in this direction. I often collapsed, and my body stayed in a freeze response way longer than needed. I shamed myself a lot during this phase, for self-sabotage and not knowing better by now. Today, I can see that this just kept me in the negative cycle of shame. I don't like the concept of self-sabotage because it comes with a taste of shame, which is unhealthy. It is actually bullshit, because why would I shame myself and keep myself small instead of acknowledging that these are old patterns and very often protective mechanisms from our nervous systems, whose only job is to keep us safe. Our job is to recognize, reteach and realign those outdated responses that keep us small. If we cannot do that by ourselves, then it is our responsibility to ask for help. It is on us to take action towards what we want.

I had to hit rock bottom the way I did to gain the learnings, insights, compassion, and wisdom I have today. Now, as I look back, I am okay with it. The reason I am sharing this is I always thought that I was alone in this struggle. The more I travel and talk to people, especially my age group, the more I see that I am not alone in this, and neither are you. I see so many lost and stuck between the old, traditional values and their inner knowing that there must be more out there. They want more in life, and they want more for their life. I guess what I am struggling with the most is that sometimes, when I feel alone with this, especially in hard times, I tend to crawl into my cave, which doesn't help because I only feel more alone. When I break that pattern, come out of my shell and start talking to new friends or people I meet along the road, I actually see that many people feel the same. It is not easy to break free from values and patterns passed onto us, especially those deep-running ones. But that is OK. It is well worth doing it anyway!

Do you feel alone in this, too?

What old, traditional values have you learned?

Which of those values no longer serve you anymore?

What patterns have you adopted from your family that no longer serve you?

Song: "This is 30" - by Loren Rosko

TWO
MY DRUMBEAT IS DIFFERENT

I GREW up in a tiny mountain village in a valley in the middle of the Austrian Alps. It is very well known for its picturesque landscapes, charming villages, traditional architecture and incredible cuisine. The valley is surrounded by gorgeous mountains and nature. The region is renowned for its rich cultural heritage, traditional craftsmanship and the preservation of local customs and traditions. This made it a great place to grow up and have a carefree childhood, always playing outdoors. Sometimes, I feel like I grew up in a movie. Like those around me, I initially followed the conventional path — starting with kindergarten, then progressing through school, high school, and eventually university. The way that was paved for me by many others. From very early on, I learned that if you want to make it in life, you need to be good in school and get good grades so you can study to get a high-paying job.

Growing up there was equally a blessing and a curse. A blessing because it was a gorgeous place surrounded by lots of nature, and I still had a childhood that I was not hijacked by social media. We spent all day outside through summer and winter, and all too often my mother had to persistently remind my brother and me to finally come inside the house for dinner or a warm cacao in winter. We grew up in the middle of a small village surrounded by many other children. We would hop on our bikes and ride up and down the village roads and collect other children to explore and play in the forest or the little creek nearby. We would run around all day, playing different games. In winter, we would spend all day playing in the snow, skiing or snowboarding, building snowmen, and sledding. I sometimes look at this part of my childhood like it was a cheesy, overly romanticized Hollywood movie. I really cherish how I grew up and the many fond memories I love to look back on. I feel very blessed to have been able to grow up in a safe environment too, where we, as children, could just roam around the village and nature without any fear that something would happen to us.

But growing up in a remote town also had its downsides. I also recall not-so-positive memories, such as being constantly reminded how to behave in public because of what other people would think. "What would the neighbors think?" As I have seen in many different, small villages around the world, people often just talk about each other in very judgmental, negative, and even envious ways sometimes. I have experienced it at home, in school, in the village in general, and in different jobs that I have had in this region. People will judge you for anything — how you dress, the job you have, and how often you go to church. Going to church was a big thing back then, and if you didn't go, it would almost be considered a scandal. Luckily, we were never really forced to go to church like others my age, but I still learned that is what you are supposed to do to be a good member of society. You go to church, confess your sins, receive absolution, and then go about living your life. I even remember the priest coming to school once a semester, so us children could confess our sins and receive absolution. As a kid, I never really understood this concept. The rebel in me didn't want to confess because I didn't think I had done anything wrong. But I also learned from an early age to be "the good girl" and comply, so I didn't have the courage to speak up for myself. I just invented stuff and never did my five prayers that I was told to do so God would give me his absolution and love me again. I would just sit and wait on a bench in the church, contemplating, "Have I been sitting here long enough now? Can I go? Would it be obvious that I haven't done my prayers?" I also thought to myself how stupid this is, me having to do something to be worthy of someone's love, even the unconditional love of God. But that is how I learned that love is not something unconditional; it is something you receive in exchange for fitting into this picture of being the good, well-behaved, less needy, quiet people pleaser.

"The good, nice and well-behaved" girl was a mask I put on, especially from an early age. You know, the one that is nice to everyone, accommodating, pleasing, not too loud, not too complicated, and would put everyone else's needs before hers.

This mask became the super chill, laid-back, cool chick in my late teenage years.

I loved it because the people in my surroundings would love me for it.

I wasn't complicated.

I wasn't needy.

I was agreeable.

I was accommodating.

I remember that I had a lot of friends who told me how they loved this side of me, that I was so easygoing and not complicated at all. I loved that! I was hungry for their approval and attention. My mantra used to be, "I don't care what we do as long as we do it together." As a result, I often found myself in situations I didn't genuinely enjoy, convincing myself that being with the person mattered more than the activity. Now I realize that though being present with someone remains important, expressing my needs and desires is equally important rather than engaging in activities I don't enjoy at all.

Looking back now, I can see that I didn't have needs. Or if I dared to have needs, I would not express them, especially if they were different from the person I was spending time with. If I dared to express them, I would be met with resistance, followed by discussions or even fights. Some friends were not used to me speaking up and possibly having to compromise at that time. I didn't learn how to have healthy conflicts or to manage conflict at all. I learned to keep the harmony, so I desperately tried to do that. Keeping the harmony, not having needs, pleasing everyone around me and accommodating their needs before mine. Needless to say, those friendships didn't last. I have needs now; I have always had them, but I don't repress them anymore. I boldly express them! It took me some time to learn to do that in a loving and kind way. I went from not expressing my needs at all to the opposite extreme of the pendulum, expressing them in a harsh and forceful manner.

I grew up in a household with my father being a vet, driving from farmer to farmer all day. My stay-at-home mother did the major part of taking care of the household, me and my brother, and managing the vet practice and in-house pharmacy. They did their best, and I am very grateful for so much they taught and generously gave me until today. But like everyone, when you don't look at the traumas and patterns you adopted from childhood and throughout your life, you unconsciously repeat them until someone breaks free. I never perceived my parents as available to lean into emotions in order to teach me how to regulate them or my nervous system. As a child, I very often felt I was an additional burden to their already stressful life and learned from an early age to keep my emotions to myself. Today, this still plays out in patterns, like withdrawing when I am feeling really sad or not asking for help and doing everything by myself, becoming hyper-independent. Learning to ask for help has been a journey for me, and it still takes a lot of effort to show up, open up, be vulnerable, and actually ask. My nervous system is wired to believe that tasks can only be done properly if I handle them myself. So changing this pattern and relearning that felt very unsafe at first, and I resisted it for a long time, also due to the deep-rooted fear of being a burden to someone else. The same goes for not feeling validated or seen in my emotions as a child. At times, when it felt too much for my parents, they told me to stop crying or sent me to my room to calm me down. So, as a child, I learned that my emotions were not welcome. I pushed them down and didn't deal with them for a long time. As I grew older, this showed up as still not being able to actually feel my emotions, but instead starting to project my fears and traumas on other people when they triggered me. As a young adult, I used to have anger issues, which would come to the surface when I drank too much alcohol. I would start to lash out, and all the repressed anger would surface all at once and be directed at the friends that I had at that time. I have lost a lot of friendships due to that.

I always had the feeling of being the black sheep in my family. The one that just does not quite fit in, never mind how hard I tried. I could not feel their drumbeat of life because mine was different. As I write this book and look back on my life and how I grew up, I know that the cycles of traumas running through my family are ending with me. My drumbeat was longing for more. Since a very early age, I wanted to be free, independent, not put into boxes or be "the good girl" and do what I have been told. My parents told me a few stories of me breaking out at a super young age already. I think I was about one and a half years old and we were at the airport in Zurich. I was standing next to my father and telling him I was going to my mother, instead I left and went on an exploration mission. I don't have any memories of that event, but knowing myself, I imagine little Claudia just wandering up and down the big airport, exploring and tasting my first steps into freedom. Meanwhile, my poor parents must have internally died about 1000 deaths until they found me a little later on one of the escalators. Another story they told me was that I would never take their hand when walking in public. I just didn't want to. I would always want to walk by myself, and one of them had to go after me all the time because I just wouldn't sit still. When we were on vacation, all my parents wanted was to sit together and have a meal in peace, but only one of them would be able to sit down and eat while the other had to run after me to watch over me while I was out and about exploring. One day, they found a cute little Italian restaurant with a fence, which enabled them to sit down and eat while being able to watch over me while I ran around in circles at the same time. Hearing this story and knowing myself, I was probably looking for an exit…haha!

I don't have a lot of conscious memories from my early childhood, but there is one clear memory from my time in kindergarten because it was such an intense feeling. When the mothers brought their children to the kindergarten, they would usually stand around and watch them because neither one of them wanted to separate yet. Not me. My mother told me when she brought me to kindergarten, I told her she could go home now. She was quite shocked and not really ready yet, but she left anyway. I also didn't want her to come and get me from kindergarten, I wanted to walk home by myself, and I am so glad she let me. She later told me she let me do that because she could watch over me the entire time walking home to our house, which was only a minute or so. The village was so small, and we lived right in the center, where everything was super close. I clearly remember this immense feeling of joy, freedom and independence. Writing these lines made me remember the liberation I felt in every fiber of my being, which actually makes me smile right now. I felt so much aliveness coming through in this little moment, and I was only four or five years old at that time.

Looking back, I have a deep knowing that is what it is all about for me in my life — feeling alive in your body, in this precious life you have right here, right now. So, this longing for freedom has been with me since a young age. In my native language, German, we have a word that captures this feeling closely. The word is "Fernweh," which literally translated means "far sickness"— kind of like feeling homesick but in reverse. I interpret that as a profound longing for distant, unknown places I have not yet visited. This can be a longing for adventures in foreign places or cultures in the world. But also a longing for distant yet unknown places within the depths of your being. A longing to go deep into our souls and begin to uncover the unconscious shadows that rule our lives until we make them conscious, accept, love and release them. This yearning is my drumbeat, beating and guiding me to follow my own "Fernweh," my own deep knowing that there has to be more to life. My drumbeat longs for aliveness, vibrancy, deliciousness, openness and magic. My drumbeat is just different from the ones around me. My drumbeat wanted more in life, even though, for a very long time, I had no idea what this was. Sometimes, I still feel I don't know, but that is absolutely ok because I am on my way. I love that my drumbeat is different. Today, I even embrace it, but it has not always been like that.

Sometimes, the drumbeat was really loud, and other times, it was just very much in the background, hardly noticeable. As I grew up and started going to school, the drumbeat got pushed more and more into the background, and my hunger for love, attention and belonging from the peers in my village came more to the forefront. As a child, you are in this super exciting bubble, everything is new and wants to be discovered. The world is endless and you feel you can do or achieve anything. If you fall, you stand up again; if something is not working out, you try a different way until it starts working out. You don't think that the world is a restricted place, nor are you afraid of failure. Actually, you feel that your possibilities are endless. I felt that. But then, as I grew up and started going to school, I started to suppress the longing for this deep freedom that made me feel so alive. As I am writing this about my early childhood, I don't remember a lot of images or situations. I remember intense feelings of true freedom and being alive that have stayed with me my entire life and guided me to this day. Looking back, going to school was quite restrictive. I had to follow all these rules because everyone else did. This longing for freedom was not welcome because it was so different. So often, I was told that I must be a good student, learn a lot and work hard if I want to make it in life. But if I look at the school system, so many different, creative young souls are put together, yet the school system makes them all learn the same stuff. Everyone is measured with the same parameters without taking the child's individuality into account. I feel like this shuts down our individuality, creativity and uniqueness and actually kills our own unique drumbeat. Especially at a young age, we are just like sponges soaking up everything we are told without discernment. Albert Einstein's quote comes to mind: "Everybody is a genius. But if you judge a fish by its ability to climb a tree, it will live its whole life believing that it is stupid." That's how I felt school was for many of us. We got measured by the lowest common dominator without embracing or considering our individuality. I feel this is a big reason this deep longing for freedom and aliveness got suppressed for quite a while. It was not welcomed by society's standards or within the school system. I do not recall anyone else in my class feeling out of the norm the same way I did, but then again, I repressed my drumbeat, so anyone who felt the same might have stifled theirs, too.

As I went through the stages of school, being treated like an outsider for most of my school life, I suppressed that feeling of being different and substituted it with the hunger of just wanting to fit in and belong. Today, I know this is a natural human desire, but I didn't realize that back then. I did anything to belong, even if it went against my inner knowing. Yet this feeling of being different and knowing there is more out there than just the paved way by society never left me. I tried to silence this little nudge deep down, which worked for a little while but came back stronger and louder than ever. Deep down, I knew the way paved for me by my family and society was not my way. I knew it would not make me happy to go down this road, but I also didn't know what else there was out there since I didn't see anyone in my surroundings breaking out of the patterns and society I grew up in. Being different is one of my greatest assets today. I want to be different because embodying my difference inspires others to do the same. We are all different, and that is something beautiful and unique. Let's bring out our uniqueness again.

What makes you different?

What makes you unique?

What is holding you back from embracing your uniqueness?

Song: "Freak" - Jeremy Loops

THREE
BREAKING FREE: STRIKE 1
SUMMER, SUN, BARCELONA

As INDIVIDUALS, we are greatly shaped by the society that we grew up in. The valley I grew up in had very strong traditional values that were still highly influenced by the church at that time. Those values can be compatible with us and what we want in life or not. For me, those values felt very often confining and it's not that they were at fault; I simply couldn't find their relevance in my life. I didn't disagree with all the values, but those that I felt negatively affected me also shaped me, my patterns, my nervous system and what I considered "normal", which actually was unhealthy for me.

I believe the people in my surroundings are very proud of their roots and have a strong sense of belonging to the place they call home. Being family-oriented is a great value. In the past, it was very common for up to three generations to live together under one roof. While today this tradition still exists, younger generations nowadays much prefer to have their own place. Being social and helpful is very important in such a small town and region where everyone knows each other. Having a good job, being actively engaged and contributing to the community by being part of different associations are highly valued. On one hand, this leads to a "hands-on" mentality, which can definitely be seen as a positive trait. In my experience, though, if you are not part of this constant doing, contributing and busyness, you would be seen as lazy. This ingrained value left very little space and allowance for just being and resting. I very often didn't allow myself to just be and rest and got caught up in the "doing" until I was exhausted. Resting, in general, was only truly accepted when you were sick, but only if you physically couldn't leave the bed. As a result, enduring pain and suffering was seen as a trait of strength. During so many episodes of my life, I have endured pain and suffering for far too long because I first told myself it wasn't that bad, I could endure. Secondly, I thought it was "normal" to suffer in life. Today, I know I don't have to endure anything that causes me more suffering than anything else. I have learned to prioritize my own well-being in choosing a healthier path, even though it hasn't always been easy. I consciously had to learn to take my time, listen to my body and give it the rest it truly needs, especially during my period. The permission to care for myself without feeling bad or selfish has become such a precious part of my life and overall health and happiness. Similar to having to consciously learn to listen to my body and choose a healthier path for myself, I had to learn what it meant to truly feel, be with, and process my emotions, especially the uncomfortable ones. I learned long ago that talking about emotions is not welcomed or encouraged, but rather should be elegantly held back under the pretense that everything is fine. One of the few values I truly cherish is the connection to nature. The incredible amount of interest, knowledge and effort surrounding protecting nature, alternative medicine using herbs, and cultivating and exchanging fruits and vegetables all resonates deeply with me. Because people are still so connected to the traditional values I just described, welcoming new ideas or alternative ways of living probably takes a lot more time than in other regions. Consequently, growing up there and feeling so different from the rest was not always the easiest experience for someone like me.

As you grow older, there are two common ways to go about life in Austria. The first one is to go to school up until 16 years old and enter an apprenticeship in a job of interest afterward, with the expectation to stay in that job until you retire. Now, this mindset is changing a bit, but very slowly. The second option is to complete high school at 18 years old and choose the area in which you want to work afterward, looking for the appropriate course of study. I hadn't a clue what I wanted at 18 years old. I struggled to choose the area in which I wanted to pursue a career. How can I make such a big decision without really having any experience in life yet? In my opinion, 18 years is too young to make such a big decision. The only thing I knew at that age was that I wanted to leave the village and the valley I grew up in. I felt trapped there, and the people seemed to have a more narrow-minded perspective on life. Others might describe them as just very traditional, which is true too. Traditional values are still very much respected there, and I am not speaking out against those values, but they were just not for me then. Some are still not to this day, although I have come to see the value in others. But at 18 years old, I wanted to break free, look for my "something more," and follow my drumbeat. Additionally, living at home with an overly protective mother was not always easy for a big freedom lover like me. Today, I understand her struggles and where she was coming from, but I did not back then. I just felt that something was holding me back, keeping me small. At the same time, I was young and too inexperienced to know what else there could be. So, struggling at home and living in a place with very traditional values and views on life that didn't suit me at all wasn't easy. From a place like this, how can you decide where you want to go in life? I definitely could not. I decided to go another route.

I had the privilege to grow up in a family that could afford to go on holidays in Spain several times a year, so from a very young age, I was immersed in other cultures. I might not have been so conscious about it growing up, but I guess it did have a big impact on me. I remember at the age of 15/16, we went to Barcelona for a few days. I loved the vibrancy of the city, as well as the aliveness, and passion of the Spanish people. It had a profound impact on me. I knew I would be coming back to this city. I wanted to explore it more and immerse myself even deeper in the dynamic energy that resonated so strongly with my inner being and yearning. I also always loved the Spanish language. I loved the rhythmic flow and the many creative and abundant ways you can describe things. I perceive the language as very artistic, passionate, creative and expressive. I love that. Up to this day, it is one of my favorite languages and no matter where I am I take every opportunity to speak it. Led by the desire to learn this language, I signed up for the Spanish course at my high school. Not only was I motivated by learning the language but also by a field trip to Spain for ten days to dive even deeper into the culture. Unfortunately, we only met once a week for two hours, which was not enough for me. I wanted more. What is the best way to learn a language? Immerse yourself in a Spanish-speaking country. That is what I did! Remembering the profound impression the city of Barcelona left on me, that was the place I chose.

I couldn't wait until my last year in high school was over. I couldn't wait until I could leave the place I grew up in. Apart from that, I was trying to repress my drumbeat, but it became louder and stronger. It was growing from a little nudge to a wrecking ball inside of me that I just couldn't ignore anymore. I am grateful that I could never silence this feeling, it prevented me from following a path not meant for me.

I was so happy when I finished high school. Once again, I felt like a free bird, ready to embark on my own journey. It was finally time for MY life to begin. I followed the path society told me so far, and now it was MY turn. I spent an amazing summer in Austria, but I also knew that I would move to Barcelona by the end of it, which made me even more excited.

This was my first attempt to break free and not do what I had been told was right for me. Those weekly two-hour Spanish classes didn't give me a good foundation for living in the country. I hardly spoke Spanish. There is a big difference between attending a language course to memorize vocabulary and phrases and living in a Spanish-speaking country and engaging in real-life conversations. Joining a language school in the beginning was very helpful and gave me a solid foundation in the language. I am very grateful that my parents supported me on this one. Even though they might not have understood why I wanted it, they had my back.

After a few months of living there, I fell in love with a man. I realized it didn't matter to me whether I worked in Spain or Austria. Can you imagine being an 18-year-old young woman living in a buzzing city for the first time by herself, with no one telling her what to do or how to do it? No trying to pressure me with their way of doing things or expecting me to fulfill any unspoken expectations? I loved it. I worked a bit and partied hard! Good times, but also a lot of learning. I had to learn how to do life, what it meant to cook for myself, wash, manage the household, and share the house with people I didn't know who came from different cultures. I learned an entirely new language and even improved my English immensely. I met so many people from different countries and cultures and learned how people with other backgrounds and values live their lives. I learned that there are so many different ways of living, which fascinated me. Before leaving Austria, I only knew one way of pursuing life, which didn't really fit me. I also couldn't put into words what I wanted to be different in my life, because, up to that point, I hadn't yet experienced something different. Being in Spain in this big, vibrant, alive and international city was truly an eye-opening experience. It literally opened me up to a whole new world and I thought, "Oh wow. I was right. There is so much more out there! I knew it!

I reconnected to my sense of feeling free and alive again, which also marked the moment I got bitten by the travel bug. My passion for traveling was born. Society's programs of being the good girl, the good student attending university because that is the only way of getting a good job and earning lots of money were still deeply rooted in my being. After one year, a sense of guilt emerged as it seemed I wasn't doing something "useful" with my life or contributing something "useful" to society. I was merely indulging in fun, partying and working just enough to sustain my lifestyle. I didn't want to give up traveling and this connection to freedom, but also felt the need to fulfill the unspoken societal expectation to do something "useful" with my life. I decided to compromise by studying tourism. This choice enabled me to continue exploring the world, having this sense of liberation, but easily finding a job in any country. Back in 2008, the concept of working online from anywhere in the world was not born yet. Subsequently, this became my version of traveling the world and working from anywhere. So that is what I did. I entered the pathway of society again, even though I knew that this was not for me and I didn't want to take on those values.

. . .

UNLEASHED

Song: "Young, Wild & Free" - Snoop Dogg, Wiz Khalifa ft. Bruno Mars

FOUR
WHEN SOCIETY'S "GOOD LIFE" DOESN'T FIT

WHAT IS "THE GOOD LIFE"?

Well, in my experience growing up, it was having stable employment, a good income, finding a partner, building a home, and having a family. This can be beautiful to have if it is true to your heart! At some point in life, I did have "the good life", or at least parts of it. I had a well-paying job in Switzerland, was living in a shared apartment with roommates that I really liked, lots of friends, and weekends filled with activities. But still, something was missing. I wanted more from life. The life I was living was not enough for me, and I actually don't like saying this. I feel ashamed and ungrateful for expressing this because I know there is so much suffering in the world and other people would give everything to have what I had. I judged myself for that and felt quite ashamed to even complain about my life. However, I realized that it doesn't help me when I compare myself to others in far worse situations because it invalidates my emotions in the present moment. A key part of my healing was to stop comparing and undermining myself and just be with what is, accepting and honoring my emotions that are presently emerging, truly feeling and letting them go.

For me, this kind of "good life" didn't feel true for a very long time. After 16 years of exploring the external world and my inner world, I desire a home base and a partner with whom I can build a life, but on my terms. I am consciously not using the words "settling down." Over the years, I have developed a resentment for those words because everyone around me wanted me to settle down way earlier than I was ready to. I can only assume it was because they wanted me near them, which is a beautiful reason. Unfortunately, I perceived it as being forced onto me as well as expected of me, influenced by societal norms that dictate when to settle down.

As you can see, I am very much against being told what to do and how to be, simply because it doesn't take my needs and desires into account. Being told what to do, how to be, and what to feel or not feel, doesn't consider what I want and need. The same applies to my family's and friend's desire for me to settle down, as I sensed that it was heavily influenced by their needs, which, in turn, were again shaped by societal norms and expectations. I was met with resistance because I was going against the grain. I was seeking alternative possibilities that go beyond the conventional way of settling down. I was seeking a different lifestyle, one that was truer to my adventurous soul. A lifestyle that doesn't imply my loss of freedom and allows me to move to my own rhythm and create my own world. The words "settling down" simply have the connotations of force, expectation, being anchored to something, and simply following the carved path. It feels limiting to me. A friend painted a beautiful picture that describes it pretty well: Imagine a child simply playing and being in pure joy and then suddenly out of nowhere someone tells the child to stop. What happens? Most likely, the child follows the command of this person and stops, but what does it do to the child? It kills the free flow and joy that the child was in and teaches them to shut off and not follow what is true to them. If this happens repeatedly, it will result in shutting them off from their authentic selves. That's pretty much what the words "settling down" invoke in me. On the other hand, the words "home base" feel more expansive, lighter, freer, while invoking a sense of stability, belonging, rootedness and a certain comfort. In essence, a more flexible and open approach: a place where I can come home to but also venture out and explore the world again if I desire. It feels more like a place of my creation than a place of enforcement.

After my year in Barcelona at 19 years old, I came home with a deep sense of being different. Something had shifted within me, though I couldn't quite pinpoint exactly what it was at the time. I refused to be forced into anything that didn't feel true to me anymore. I no longer wanted to be available for that anymore. Despite being accepted and supported by my friends for who I am and wish to become, I still haven't had the sense of being truly understood, and this left me feeling quite lonely for a long time. Due to growing up with those traditional values, the program of following "the good life" was running deep through me and kept me doubting my life choices over and over again. After several exploring escapades, I would return to Austria again and again to follow the path intended for me by society. I actually tried to fit in several times, but it was never quite right and the more I forced it, the more I felt like life was being sucked out of me. It truly felt like every day I was becoming smaller and smaller instead of growing and stepping into my power.

One of the main reasons I came back from Barcelona was that I felt I maybe should do something "useful" with my life, and I started looking for tourism studies in Austria. I found the "Tourismuskolleg Innsbruck," a two-year school offering subjects like Marketing, Language, Hospitality, Accounting, and many others. This school perfectly fit my internal compromise of doing something that society considered "useful" while also allowing me to continue traveling and working in different countries. Because working online wasn't really a thing back in 2008, I did my studies and embarked on another adventure in beautiful Italy to work. I wanted to learn Italian and thought, "Well, learning Spanish in Spain without much knowledge worked out pretty well, so it will work out in Italy too." And it did! After the first month, which was quite challenging, I picked up Italian pretty quickly and had a great time. Once again, I felt closer to myself than at home, even though I was 20 and had no idea about personal development. I just wanted to enjoy myself and be in an energy that did not require me to fulfill any unspoken expectations.

After two years at Innsbruck, I did what I thought I needed to do to live a successful life. I got my Bachelor's degree in Tourism and Marketing, which is often required for higher-level job applications. I applied to different universities in Europe and got accepted to one in Switzerland. My thought was simply, "OK, let's move to Switzerland then" without big excitement, but rather a sense of acceptance that this is what I needed to do. In hindsight, I always knew this was not my path, but I did it anyway. It again gave me a deep sense of belonging to a group of peers I was so desperately looking for. It also gave me some sort of purpose, structure and plan for the next few years. Most importantly, it served as an excuse to avoid confronting my inner drumbeat, which was so different from the path I was on. It was simply too painful to look at, and my hunger for acceptance and belonging was intense at that time. So once again, I tried to suppress my drumbeat, but it never entirely left me alone. It was always lingering in the background until one day, I had the idea of venturing again to South America. I still had a few years left in university, but now I had something to look forward to, which gave me a sense of excitement like a light at the end of the tunnel.

Because Switzerland is quite an expensive country to live in, I worked a lot to afford living there, and saved as much as possible for my upcoming trip. I worked several jobs throughout my studies and even had a regular job afterward, working weekends to save as much money as possible so I could travel without worry. I had to be smart in saving and spending my money. I was in my early 20s and loved going out, having fun and enjoying myself, so the next logical thing was to work in a club instead of going out and spending my money there. I would be in the same fun, energetic atmosphere but also earning money. I had a lot of fun and really loved it. After my studies, I landed a very good marketing job but continued to work in the club. Instead of living alone, I shared an apartment with three other people.

Here I was, ticking many societal boxes: high-profile job, earning well, lots of friends, and living in a nice apartment. I was only missing a partner to tick all the boxes. I have to admit, for a while, it felt really good! I was valued and appreciated in my job, I got along with my work colleagues, and my boss encouraged and challenged me to grow. I would say that was the only employment position that I truly enjoyed. After a year in my marketing job, I became bored as the work I once enjoyed became repetitive and lacked challenges.

My weekends were filled with leisure activities I planned weeks ahead. Whenever I wanted to meet with certain friends, I had to plan to see them 4-6 weeks in advance. In my experience, Swiss people generally like to be very busy and active, so spontaneity was, unfortunately, rarely possible. I was only 25, but looking at my calendar left me feeling more stress than joy, and deep down, I knew that this wasn't what I wanted for the rest of my life. Even though my calendar was filled with lots of pleasurable things to do, I lacked spontaneity and time by myself. There was only room for everything else — work, friends, events, parties, weekend get-a-ways. Like my surroundings, I was infected by the constant energy of doing and being active, driven by the fear of missing out on life otherwise. There was the underlying drumbeat that did not let me be at peace, in fact, it got louder every day. I saved every penny I could. At high peak times, I was working three jobs, but it didn't matter because this yearning to leave and the calling to go to South America was so loud that everything else was secondary. And in 2015, I did it. I remember it was Friday, May 23, and I was leaving my office with a bittersweet feeling of leaving behind something good I created for myself, but I was super excited about what was to come. I spent almost two years in South America and had the time of my life, reconnecting to parts of myself that were hidden deep, deep down, that I didn't even know existed back then. Once again, I left "the good life" behind and created my own path by diving deep into South American culture. I intended to go for about six months or so, but it somehow became almost two years. I left at 25 years old, sensing that this was still an acceptable age to take some time to travel and explore, but the expectation of me coming back to follow the conventional path was always lingering in the background. To return, land a good paying job, find an apartment, and start ticking societal boxes - finding a partner, creating a family, and buying a home. Although I knew these expectations would be waiting for me, I didn't care at the time. I just wanted to leave and live without having those expectations dangling over my head. I would deal with those later.

UNLEASHED

What do you feel when thinking about "settling down"?

What do you feel when thinking about "the good life"?

What is missing for you?

Song: "Rebel" - Sean Koch

FIVE
BREAKING FREE: STRIKE 2
REKINDLING MY FEMININE SIDE

WHAT I REALLY LOVE ABOUT traveling, apart from experiencing new cultures, meeting new people, trying new food, and just simply being yourself outside your usual surroundings is the opportunity to explore new aspects within yourself. Traveling solo shows you how capable you are in many different situations because there is no other choice. You must resolve problems by yourself, speak up, and stand up for yourself. And you do because there is simply no other way. It is a journey to self-discovery and empowerment. I can totally relate to that. Traveling by myself opened up the space to become more authentically myself without the weight of pre-existing roles and expectations from friends and family. Strangers didn't see me as the people pleaser or the good girl I was at home, enabling me to express myself more freely and with less resistance. My first big solo travel trip to South America in 2015 & 2016 was a profound journey of self-discovery. I gained valuable insights about myself, transforming my life forever.

I learned how capable I am and how strong I can be if I need to.

I learned not to let people walk over me.

I learned to speak up for myself and for what I want.

I learned to resolve problems quickly and often on my own.

I learned to be more courageous.

I learned to be more resilient.

I learned to trust.

I learned that there are other sides in me that have been dormant for almost my entire life because they had no space to emerge in Austria.

Even though I lived in Barcelona and Italy at a very young age, my journey to South America truly initiated me into a deeper connection to myself. I was 25 and somewhat wiser than I was at 18, but not yet connected to my spirituality and intuition. I underwent a powerful initiation into embracing my feminine side more, exploring my sensuality and reconnecting to my sexuality. It allowed me to soften the hard shell I had built over the years. At home, being overly sexual was seen as sinful and would lead to being severely judged and almost being canceled, so my sensual, sexual side had no space there. Harsh judgment would already start with wearing seemingly wrong clothes. Wearing a summer dress with high heels was already deemed scandalous.

The profound transformation I undertook in South America forged a deep and lasting connection with that part of the world up until today. I am in awe of their rich culture, deep sense of living in tune with nature, and their naturally deep connection with spirit and the Universe. I feel honored that I could visit several different countries and that so many people there have shared their ancient wisdom with me in one form or another. I remain deeply touched by this truly magical place, and have felt called to go back there many times.

I still vibrantly remember the day I left my office in Switzerland and knew that within a few days I would finally fulfill my big dream of exploring South America, a dream I had been working towards for a few years. Finally, the day arrived and I was leaving the only employment that I enjoyed in my life. I didn't intend to leave after only 1.5 years, but my contract wasn't extended, so the decision was made for me. Looking back, I am grateful for this intervention, as I am unsure if I would have left at that time on my own. My life started to become very comfortable and I fell into the pattern of doing what everyone else around me was doing. I'm grateful that the decision was made for me, as I believe the Universe was guiding me toward something more aligned with my true self. It turned out to be a blessing. As I left, there was both the feeling of joy and sadness, but honestly, joy outweighed the rest. I vividly remember the moment even now - I was walking out of the office with the song "Au Revoir" by German Artist "Mark Foster" and "Sido" in my ears and feeling immensely free and liberated. I had the biggest smile on my face and was just thinking, "Hell yeah, let's do this." At that moment, I felt like my real life was about to begin. The song captured this feeling beautifully - the artists are tired of the same monotonous routine in their lives, expressing the desire for something more. Motivated by a deep longing for freedom and adventure, they leave their old life behind and embark on a journey to explore the world, and find new experiences and a sense of freedom. I was listening to this song for months before I left and it deeply resonated with me, expressing what I felt and my longing for freedom. I left three days later, on the 25th of May 2015, for Bolivia. My first big solo trip, going overseas without any particular plan or end date. I was filled with a mix of excitement and terror at the same time. I was about to embark on a whole new journey to a whole new continent and culture that I didn't know much about. In preparation, I immersed myself for almost an entire year in all the travel blogs in German and English that I could find, absorbing the information like a sponge. I researched packing lists, safety tips, and video blogs to prepare myself as well as possible. However, I could not ignore the fear that wasn't entirely my own. At the time, I was still following the news and, to a certain extent, was more open to being influenced by other people's opinions. We all know the media is not the most positive source of information. Unfortunately, South America didn't receive the best media coverage in Europe.

An interesting observation I made of many people in my surroundings is that they seemed to have strong opinions of those countries despite having little travel experience. They very often relied on hearsay or the news as their source of information. Let me tell you, there is a big difference between hearing about a country and experiencing it firsthand. Before I left, I heard a lot of negative information, mostly about kidnapping, theft, and murder, very often in combination with having to be super careful as a woman traveling alone with countless restrictions on what I should or shouldn't do and places I should avoid. While it's important to be careful when traveling solo, in my experience, there is a fine line between being cautious and discerning and between being afraid and holding yourself back. In this case, I would say to simply trust your gut. If something doesn't feel right, there is no need to look for a reason or a justification. Just trust that feeling.

Before I left, I was trying to focus on the positive aspects of my journey by reading all the wonderful things about the vibrant, culturally rich, and colorful nature of those countries with open, expressive and passionate people. Yet, while I was sitting on the airplane bound for Bolivia, a little voice of fear was lingering in the back of my head. Deep down, I knew that this was not entirely my voice, and I am grateful that I didn't let myself be held back by that. When I arrived in La Paz in Bolivia, I was simultaneously super excited and nervous. I had pre-booked accommodation online for the first three nights, including airport transportation, as I wanted to arrive safely at my hostel, especially since I was arriving in the middle of the night. From back home, I had the feeling to double-check the airport transportation, but I didn't listen to this gut feeling and convinced myself that everything would be fine. At that time, it was hard to distinguish if this was my intuition or fear. On the airplane, I again sensed the same doubts emerging about my airport transfer. However, as I am generally afraid of flying, being nervous on airplanes was nothing unusual, so I convinced myself that those feelings were just my fear of flying instead of my intuition. As I arrived at the airport, I realized that my airport transfer didn't show up. My intuition was right all along. I found myself standing in a small airport in a dodgy neighborhood in La Paz. I couldn't call anyone, and I thought, "Shit, what am I going to do now?" Now, all the negative comments I heard were rushing through my head and a slight feeling of panic was sneaking in. All the other passengers from my airplane already left, and I found myself alone with a few shady men who kept staring over at me all the time, leaving me feeling very uncomfortable. There was no one else around, no taxis waiting outside the airport, nothing. With no other solution, my only option was to remain at the airport and wait for the next airplane to arrive. I hoped for someone who had organized an airport transfer and would be kind enough to take me with them. I waited about two hours, which seemed like the longest two hours of my life. I was super tired, jetlagged and highly uncomfortable due to those men lingering around the airport, who kept looking over at me, talking and laughing. I can only assume they were talking about me. At that time, I was not really into praying, but I kept wishing for them to leave me alone. As the next airplane arrived, I desperately scanned for someone who looked kind enough to take me to the city's center. I spotted another backpacker waiting outside for a car, so I gathered all my courage and approached him before it would be too late. Back then, I was still fairly shy and approaching someone else, especially men and in a foreign language, took a lot of courage from my side. However, the only other choice would have been to stay longer at the airport with those old guys constantly checking me out. I approached him and explained my situation, that I had organized a transport which never showed up and left me stranded alone at the airport and that I was hoping he could take me to town. I was extremely relieved as the guy and his driver turned out to be very kind and gave me a ride. They drove me around town for more than an hour in the middle of the night, helping me to find my hostel. They even insisted on bringing me to the door and waiting with me to be let inside, as La Paz at night can be quite dangerous. The night guard initially did not want to let me in despite having a reservation, but with the driver's persistence, I was finally allowed inside. I felt a mix of relief and concern, thinking to myself, "Oh boy, I hope this gets better." It was not the most pleasant start to my first big solo trip. Reflecting on it now, I realize that I was immediately thrown into the deep end with plans not working out as expected, leading me to learn to take immediate action and resolve any upcoming problems. I learned to overcome my shyness and fear of rejection and trust that things would work out, which has led me to kind and nice men who helped me in my situation.

Further down the line, things got significantly better and I enjoyed myself a lot, traveling around Bolivia and Peru. Many situations and challenges required me to step up for myself during my travels, but with every situation I gained more confidence and became more assertive. Unfortunately, I experienced many situations in which men would tell me what I could or couldn't do simply because I am a woman, as they believed I was unworthy. But I also encountered many kind, generous, and genuinely helpful people who went out of their way to assist me and ensure that I would have a good experience in their country. Another important skill I learned during my travels is to ask for what I want and need clearly. I was pleasantly surprised how effortlessly I would receive what I asked for. Being confident in my request, I experienced very little resistance; more often than not, people would offer their help.

After about four months of traveling in Peru, Bolivia and a bit in Ecuador, I started feeling weary and overwhelmed with the constant change and input of new experiences. After a while, being on the road, changing location every four to five days, taking another night bus, dealing with significant altitude changes, and constantly adapting to new environments and adventures became draining at the pace I was going. Around 4-5 months into my travels, I arrived at this one hostel in Quito, the capital of Ecuador, which would later become my home. Friends from Austria were coming to visit me in Ecuador, and we arranged to meet up in this hostel. It quickly became our "home base" in Ecuador due to its central location and enjoyable atmosphere. We all really liked the place, people, and overall vibe, making it a perfect spot to gather and create lasting memories. After my friends left, I started connecting more with the people working at the hostel, and due to its nice, homey and warm atmosphere, I wanted to stay longer. I truly wanted to immerse myself more in Ecuador's culture and get to know that beautiful country. I applied to volunteer at the reception and signed up for one month in exchange for accommodation and food. About two weeks into my time as a volunteer, the boss asked if I would be interested in staying and working full-time as a receptionist. I took a moment and thought to myself, "Why not? If not now, when?" It felt like an opportunity I shouldn't let slip away, so I decided to take the chance. There is no better time than now! At the same time, I didn't want to return to

Europe, returning to the same monotonous rhythm I just left behind. My body would tense up at the mere thought of going back home. Suddenly, I found myself working in a hostel surrounded by incredible people and having the time of my life. Within a few months, I found myself managing the entire place. Embracing the same thought of, "If not now, when?" I poured my heart and soul into the hostel, trying to create the most awesome experiences for travelers by sharing my passion for travel and my love for Ecuador. The time in the hostel was truly one of the best times of my life. We created a beautiful community with the people I worked with, and I felt a strong sense of belonging. Even today, I maintain close friendships with people who worked at the hostel, were guests, or lived in Quito during that time. Looking back, one aspect stands out - immersing myself in Ecuador surrounded by people who are naturally more connected to their sensuality and sexuality has led me to embrace and connect more with my own feminine, sensual and sexual side. I also perceived the Latin people as way more passionate, affectionate, expressive and emotional. Seeing this, I also wanted to connect more to those sides of my being. I wanted to be more open myself. Just being in this kind of energy had a huge effect on me, and I slowly started to open myself up to those aspects of my life.

Being surrounded by so many heart-warming and open people, I began to let my guard down and open my heart. Going out dancing helped me immensely in opening up and connecting more to my feminine and sensual side. If you have ever been to Latin America or a Latin party, you know that the Latin people are very passionate and expressive dancers with lots of hip and pelvic floor movement. I began to adopt their style and learned to move my hips more too, which initially was not easy for me due to not being used to it. Frankly, I was quite stiff. Since then, dancing has become an important part of my life, bringing me joy and happiness, deepening my connection to my intuition, igniting my fire within, inviting more creativity and transforming my mood. Especially for us women, I feel it is important to move our hips and pelvis in order to reconnect with our womb space, as it is the seat of our power. Within our womb space lies our sensuality, sexuality and eroticism, which, in essence, is our vital energy, our creativity and life force. It is also where our intuition resides. The more we get those juices flowing and connect to our body, the more we feel connected to ourselves and the flow of life.

As I embraced dancing and moving my hips more, rekindling my sensuality and sexuality, I began to shed layers of my shyness and invite my more seductive side, which had been dormant for too long. I remember a situation where a few friends and I were sitting at the big communal table on the third floor of the hostel, where the reception was. We would gather to hang out for breakfast and dinner and playfully evaluate the men coming through the door. We would rate them and jokingly decide who would take them home for some fun later that night. During that time, my friends gave me the nickname "La Tigresa," meaning "the tigress," because of my charming and seductive nature that seemed irresistible to men. Seducing men had become like a game of collecting trophies, and I took pride in being able to play with men like this. It fulfilled my desire to be admired and seen as beautiful, seductive and feminine. Ultimately, I was craving validation, especially from men. During that period, I felt very feminine, sensual and sexual, which I used to my advantage to get what I wanted, not only with men but also in life. Looking back at this time now, I can see how I had swung to the other extreme of the pendulum, from suppressing those aspects to using and manipulating them for my own personal gain. I was in the deep shadow side of the dark feminine, which is a distorted and unbalanced version and expression of femininity. As I have grown and gained more self-awareness, I have learned to embrace the light and the darkness of the feminine, finding a balance within myself.

Writing these last few paragraphs took so much effort and brought up so much resistance. Opening up and sharing this part of my life that I rarely shared with anyone made me, on the one side, smile because I remember so many fun moments that I cherish. On the other side, my fear of being rejected and harshly judged has been triggered big time. I used to carry so much shame for having had so many different sexual partners and engaging in all sorts of sexual experiences. For a long time, I felt so incredibly guilty about it, knowing that in this patriarchal world, a woman with multiple sex partners is being shamed and deemed undesirable. Especially where I grew up, strongly influenced by traditional views and the church, there was the connotation that a woman with numerous sexual partners was doomed to go to hell. I went through a phase of intense self-shame and immense guilt, at some points I was disgusted with myself. Can you imagine that? How deeply ingrained those patriarchal patterns must be to make one feel disgusted by one's actions and choices.

Today, I look back at this version of myself and feel a lot of love and compassion. I can see how deeply this old and frankly outdated pattern was running through me. Meanwhile, I've started to connect more with myself, my body, my sensuality, and my pleasure, realizing that my sexuality and pleasure are inherent rights. Today, I look back on those memories with love and a smile, and I'm not afraid to share them with others when the topic comes up. Looking back on those patterns and the unhealthy aspects of the distorted feminine that were once present in me has shaped me into the person I am today. I own and take responsibility for every "fucked up" decision, trying to do better every day. I'm proud of the person I have become through this journey of self-discovery. Honestly, looking back at the time in Ecuador makes me smile and cherish those memories. I had such a deep sense of freedom, shedding layers and masks I no longer needed. I felt so deeply connected to a more authentic version of myself with my heart wide open. However, I must say, I wouldn't want to repeat that episode of my life. It was very transformative and I took many lessons from it that greatly shaped me. But today, I am embracing new experiences and growing into a more balanced and healthier version of my feminine, sensual and sexual side.

What parts of yourself are waiting to be awakened?

When was the last time you connected to your sensuality?

Do you feel shame around expressing your sensuality/sexuality?

Song: "Au Revoir" by Mark Foster and Sido

SIX
IT IS OK TO FALL AND ASK FOR HELP

AFTER 18 MONTHS, my time in South America, and especially in Ecuador, came to an end. Apart from having the time of my life there, I had also taken over as the hostel manager for several months while my boss was away. As I mentioned, I loved this place so much that I poured my heart and soul into it. When he came back and saw the changes I initiated and what I put in motion, I was stunned to receive only accusations and complaints about what I had done wrong or wasn't good enough. Unfortunately, I didn't receive one positive word about all the work and effort I put into this place. I loved this place so much, so receiving so much negative feedback really crushed my soul and deeply hurt me. Reflecting on it, I can only assume he was terrified that I would take away his "baby." After all, the hostel was his creation and he had invested a lot of money, time, and effort, living through many ups and downs. Witnessing someone put in so much dedication and effort and doing a really good job possibly made him feel threatened and his protection mechanism activated, leading him to try to put me down. Not long after, I left completely devastated, feeling like an utter failure. Lost and left without any energy or motivation to continue my travels, I decided to return to Austria. I didn't know where else to go and my mother offered to take care of me, which, in this vulnerable moment, I openly accepted. I felt so depleted and just wanted to receive some love and a sense of being taken care of. Simultaneously, I felt like a failure, being back home at 27 years old and sitting in my old childhood room, not exactly where I imagined myself at this age.

I was deeply unhappy and overwhelmed with all my emotions that I never learned to process properly. There was a time that led me to question my whole life. I went down a rabbit hole of victimization and feelings of not being good enough, of failure, and being insanely stuck and constantly doubting my choices. The experience in Ecuador completely threw me off. On top of that, coming home from a long journey or living abroad is difficult and something very few people talk about. As I mentioned earlier, traveling opens up time and the space to truly reflect on what you want in life. It allows you to rediscover or reconnect to aspects of yourself that may have been buried in your unconscious or suppressed due to not being accepted in our society. After having experienced so much growth, transformation and rediscovery within myself in South America, returning home to a rather conservative and seemingly opposite perspective and way of life felt like a huge slap in the face. After the initial weeks of excitement of simply being happy to be back and seeing friends and family again, I started to crumble slowly. The changes I had undergone on my travels, meeting so many genuine people who welcomed me with their hearts wide open, had a profound impact on me and led to me opening my heart as well. Returning to Austria and suddenly finding myself in an emotionally cold environment again, I literally could feel my heart gradually begin to close up again. The walls of protection and shame that broke down in South America thanks to the heartwarming kindness and openness of the people I met there started to build up again. Feeling lost and stuck without any idea of what was next for me or where I wanted to go in life, I found myself again surrounded by family and friends telling me to go right back to getting a job, renting an apartment, and living my life as if nothing had changed. Once again, I felt deeply misunderstood by my surroundings, but I don't blame them. They grew up in the same society I did, not knowing anything else, and at the same time, they chose this path for themselves. While some are truly happy with this choice, I can see that some are not. Surrounded by this energy, I was full of doubt about my life choices and thought, "Maybe this is the path I was supposed to follow? Maybe it's time to settle down now. "Get back to the seriousness of life," that's how I felt. I had my fair share of wild, crazy fun, and now I felt the pressure to "get my shit together." So, I did what I was told to do and what I also felt I was supposed to do internally.

I looked at jobs in marketing, tourism and hospitality, basically anything that would give me some sort of purpose and enough money to survive. I got a job as a waitress at a restaurant up in the mountains. I loved the hours, as 9-5 was very uncommon in hospitality, but I didn't like anything else about it. The team was an interesting mix of deeply hurt people in one spot. There were many fights as we didn't get along very well and constantly projected our traumas onto each other. It was a very toxic place, but I didn't recognize that at the time. In my almost ten years of experience in hospitality, I rarely encountered a healthy work environment, so I perceived it as normal. During my time in the restaurant, I faced being sexually harassed by my boss, which I let happen because I was too afraid to speak up and say something then. Fortunately, it was only sexual comments on my appearance and never more. Deep down, I knew this was a toxic place, but I didn't feel worthy enough to make any changes and look for something better. I kept convincing myself that it wasn't so bad, while at the same time dying inside every day a little more. Alcohol became a major coping strategy for me during that time, and I would find myself drinking almost every day.

My only light during this dark time was being part of the local scouts group. Being around those kids and witnessing their pure and authentic joy brought me so much happiness. Every Thursday evening, we would gather for 1.5 hours, spending all our time outside, teaching them various things through fun and engaging games. Playing with them and seeing their faces light up was nourishment to my soul as well as my inner child. I cherished those 1.5 hours; it was the best part of my entire week, something I looked forward to each time. I had a deep sense of being part of something beautiful. A wonderful group that enjoyed spending time together in nature and possibly one of the few things that kept me going during that difficult period. While at the restaurant, I started dating one of the cooks there. Deep down, I knew that this was not a healthy connection. From the moment we started dating, and for the seven months we stayed together, I had this strong sense in my core that it wasn't right for me. I ignored my intuition, being still deeply hurt and extremely love- and attention-deprived. I would have done anything to get some sort of validation from anyone. Once again, I was ruled by the pattern of wanting to belong instead of truly trusting myself. All my friends were in stable relationships and I wished the same for myself. I didn't want to be labeled as the forever single friend. I wanted to fit into the group of being in a relationship to avoid the shame associated with "still" being single because being single for an extended time was not widely accepted. I have heard that my standards are too high too many times. Today, I firmly believe they should be high because I would rather stay alone than waste my time with someone who is not a true match. Back then, I felt so lost and stuck that I was more prone to the influence of my surroundings. I found myself trying to build a relationship with a man that I actually didn't like. Even though every fiber in my being despised him, I stayed for seven months.

Experiencing an abusive relationship made me realize how difficult it can be to leave that kind of situation. After the initial love bombing phase, to which my vulnerable and hurt self was very open, his behavior turned very quickly. He began to devalue me, giving me the sense of never being good enough for him. He started controlling me through emotional manipulation like disrespect, emotional blackmail, and gaslighting, forcing me to have sex with him. The constant cycle of being love bombed and then pushed away, put on a pedestal only to be devalued seconds later if I didn't fit his ideal image, created a toxic and confusing dynamic. The most challenging part in leaving such a relationship is that if you grew up in an emotionally similar environment, your nervous system is attuned to that. My nervous system associated this form of emotional manipulation with giving and retrieving love as one pleases, which made it difficult to see this unhealthy dynamic and eventually break free. My intuition had been whispering since the moment we met that I was only doing this because I didn't want to be alone. I desperately wanted to fit into the societal norm of being a "grown-up" with a proper job, good income, an apartment, and a partner. My body began to rebel because I did not listen to my intuition. Yeast infections were not a common issue for me before, so looking back, I can see how my body rejected him long before my mind realized.

I was engaging in other bad habits, like drinking lots of alcohol and eating unhealthy food way before I ended this relationship. I started drinking a lot every day to cope with my situation. Working in hospitality, where I was constantly surrounded by alcohol and people who would invite me for drinks didn't help the situation either. It would give me an excuse to start drinking during the day without feeling guilty. Since I was being invited and wasn't drinking alone, I convinced myself this was totally ok. I also drank a lot with him because he had the same habit, which gave me another excuse to cope with uncomfortable situations and feelings I did not want to face. However, the alcohol only dragged me down further and left me feeling even more depleted and down the next day. At a certain point, I got so desperate that I would find myself repeatedly sitting in my car driving over a bridge and wondering, "What if I just turned right here and drove over the edge." In other situations, I would find myself driving 140 km/h on the highway and contemplating, "Should I just drive into the crash barrier so that my car would roll over?" But then I worried that it might not kill me and instead just leave me paralyzed for the rest of my life. Luckily, I never did it! I was too afraid and didn't want to do this to my family or friends. There was still a thin thread of life force in me, telling me to keep fighting, this was not the end. But the thought of ending it all and being free crossed my mind more than once. Deep down I knew this man was dragging me down into this big black hole.I literally could see a black spiral before my eyes that I was dragged into, showing me how bad things had become. I knew I needed to end this situation. The breaking point came when he literally said to me: "I don't respect you, and I never will. I don't respect anyone except my mother!" These words brought such an immense shock to my system that it woke me up from this nightmare. This moment struck me like lightning and brought so much clarity that I couldn't endure this anymore, so I gathered all my courage, overcame my fear of being punished, and ended the relationship. At first, he didn't want to let me go and kept bothering me long after I ended things. Luckily, I was so sick of his behavior that I stood my ground and set firm boundaries. I was grateful that I escaped this toxic situation, yet I still felt lost and empty inside. I was still in this black spiral that he dragged me in, and I knew I couldn't get out of it on my own. To gain some clarity on what to do next, I needed time and distance. So, I took two weeks off, packed my racing bike, flew to Barcelona, and just went biking, motivated by the deep urge to just move. I had no fixed plans, I simply knew I wanted to head south. I knew the sea must always be on my left side. That was my very basic plan as I landed in Spain, and everything else I figured out day by day. Moving and sweating it all out felt so incredibly good and liberating. I treated myself to really good food and nice hotels along the way. This trip provided the necessary space and time to contemplate how I wanted to move on with life. It was also during this trip that I consciously decided that in order to improve my life and get out of this black hole I fell into, I needed professional help. This decision resonated with every fiber in my body as something I needed to do for my own well-being. Even though my mind tried to create shame around asking for help, labeling it as a sign of weakness and associating therapy with being for "crazy" people, I knew deep down that it was the right step for me. As always, the universe has my back and conspired in me meeting my first coach on a random picnic in Germany, hosted by one of my favorite German travel bloggers back then. This marked the beginning of a deeper layer of self-discovery than I had experienced so far. She came into my life at the perfect moment and turned out to be the perfect fit for me. We connected during the event, and she gave me her card to stay in contact. I was moving back and forth for about two months, unsure about contacting her. I knew I needed help to improve my life but the shame of asking for help was deep-seated. Throughout my life, my emotions were not welcome most of the time, which led me to create a protective shell that I would crawl into whenever an uncomfortable emotion arose. Reaching out and asking for help took an incredible amount of effort and courage but I am so glad I did! Working with her was a true blessing and a deeper initiation into the world of personal development and spirituality. We worked together for about six months and unraveled a lot of codependent patterns I adopted from early childhood. With her help, I made significant life changes. I left my toxic job and apartment and went to a yoga retreat in Mexico, which became a profound experience for my personal growth. Since then, I have worked with many different coaches and learned to embrace asking for help and receiving support. I realized that I don't have to do everything by myself anymore, which has been a deep-running pattern of control. Asking for help is still not always easy, but I now see the value in having an objective person holding space for me, providing insights, mirroring what is going on and asking the right questions. Today, I no longer run away from uncomfortable situations and love the transformation that comes from being helped.

How do you deal with uncomfortable emotions?

How do you feel about asking for help?

Song: "High Hopes" - Panic at the Disco

SEVEN
BREAKING FREE: STRIKE 3
ALTERNATIVE COMMUNITY LIVING GONE WRONG

THE YOGA RETREAT in Mexico opened my eyes to another unknown world for me. The three-week course was incredibly intense and brought so much revelation and learning. We dove deep into the history and philosophy of yoga, did meditation, long meditative hatha yoga classes, and even a 10-day Silent Meditation Retreat. It was quite a sobering experience on multiple levels, with many challenging but also blissful moments. One of the most beautiful aspects of the retreat was the people I met. They were genuinely kind and open-hearted. I formed some lifelong friendships. Being part of this community allowed me to be brutally honest and vulnerable, opening my heart in ways I had never done before. I learned to embrace my emotions and allow myself to truly feel. I learned to lower my guard and let people in more deeply. A quite transformative experience for me was accepting and receiving physical touch from others, as touching and hugging people was very common in this yoga community. It was quite challenging as I grew up in an emotionally cold environment where physical affection was almost non-existent, and I developed an aversion to touch. Learning to invite physical touch that was not connected or restricted to romantic partners, and becoming comfortable with it was a big breakthrough for me. Immersing myself in a community in which it was just normal and a natural part of life was extremely helpful and healing. Today, I try to embrace it whenever I can because we are humans and we need physical affection as much as we need air, food and water to survive. The more I engaged in the yoga community in Mexico, the more I fell in love with the alternative lifestyle, it being so different from what I had seen so far. I met many like-minded souls who wanted to escape the restrictive view of Western society and embrace an alternative way of living — living life with an open heart and taking communal well-being into account. I loved that! Having grown up and lived in Western countries, where individualism is highly valued and praised, being part of a community that focused on cooperation instead of constant competition brought me a lot of comfort. After two months of immersing myself in such a different and alternative lifestyle, I had to return to Europe, but this experience profoundly impacted me.

In Europe, I refused to return to the same life I left before going to Mexico. I wanted to immerse myself deeper into this alternative, spiritual, and communal living I had discovered in Mexico. I found out that the Yoga Center I had been to in Mexico had a branch in France. They had a volunteer program that offered a three-months "Karma Yoga" program in exchange for a free yoga course, a 10-day Silent Meditation Retreat, food and accommodation. Without hesitation, I applied for the program, got accepted, and was beyond excited to live in a yoga center in a gorgeous Chateau in the French Alps. As I arrived, I found a vibrant community of about 40 people of all ages running the Yoga Retreat Center and living outside of societal norms. My inner rebel loved it! Finally, I found a place with like-minded people, satisfying my need for being seen and belonging, at least for a little while. The first three months flew by quickly. I joined the community in July 2019, and we had a beautiful summer. We would gather at the big tables or in the green grass in the front yard, eating, laughing, chatting and singing together. I absolutely loved it! Spending time with such wonderful people who shared similar interests, practicing yoga, meditation, art, personal development, and simply being there for each other filled me with joy. During that time, I was going through a break-up with the first kind, genuine and loving man I had ever met, and it was hard. We met in Mexico after my abusive relationship. However, the people I had just met in the community were there for me, holding space for all my emotions and showering me with so much love. It was a new and eye-opening experience to see how life could be and how we could treat each other with compassion. It felt incredibly refreshing to be surrounded by people who encouraged me to feel my emotions without shame or judgment but with support and understanding. It took a bit of time for me to open up and show my more vulnerable side, but seeing the authentic connections and support among the community members inspired me to do the same. It felt like a safe space to be myself. After my three months came to an end, I had the possibility to extend my stay, which I gratefully took. I even signed up to be one of the long-term volunteers for an entire year, and I was beyond joyful. I felt like I had joined another special club, satisfying my hunger for belonging once more. In the beginning, I loved my life there. I was part of the marketing and kitchen teams, which was the perfect balance between office and hands-on work. I made some lifelong friends during my time there.

But at some point, it took a turn. Initially, the agreement was to work five hours a day for five days, which I was happy with. But gradually, additional chores were added under the guise of "the path of selfless service." Initially, I didn't mind at all as I loved helping the community grow so more people could benefit from this place. I really loved the vision and wanted to contribute to that. As the days got longer and the tasks seemed endless, I began to feel more exhausted and overwhelmed than anything else. At first, I was happy to contribute, but as soon I started to feel I had to fulfill these unspoken expectations and that I had to be available all the time in service to the community, I felt deeply triggered. It reminded me of trauma from my upbringing when I was always expected to be available for my family's needs. Whenever I rebelled or refused, I experienced emotional manipulation that made me feel guilty and ashamed for not being at their disposal and for wanting time to myself.

It started to feel like that in the community, so I began to pull back and became unavailable most of the time, leading to me being emotionally manipulated into guilt and shame again. The issue was addressed almost weekly during the community meetings. We were expected to fulfill those tasks to keep the place running smoothly. I knew I had to listen to my own needs and set boundaries to protect myself from feeling overwhelmed and controlled. It wasn't just me; I saw the retreat pattern in many of the long-time volunteers as they started to take more personal time. Additionally, the limited living space of up to four of us sharing a room meant we were constantly surrounded by others, which could be a bit much at times. The only time I truly had alone was when I went for long walks in the woods or exploration drives around the area. I love being with people, but I equally need time and space for myself as well. Living and serving in a Yoga Retreat Center, where people come to heal and process their life experiences can also be heavy and overwhelming, without breaks. While working on yourself, working through your own trauma is essential. We also need to have fun in life and take a step back from the intensity. After a few months, I started to lack the simple joy of having fun. Living with more than 40 people on the premises and sometimes hosting up to 100 guests, there was always someone going through something, and conversations revolved around spiritual and personal development topics all the time. It felt like the fun was taken out of life; everything always became serious. So, I rebelled and started leaving the center almost every day to do different things, sometimes alone and sometimes with friends. It felt liberating to break free from the seriousness and judgment to enjoy "worldly things" like non-vegan food, drinks, and live music without feeling like they weren't spiritual enough.

As members of the spiritual community, we had to commit to fulfilling specific daily practices. These included attending daily morning meditation at 7 am and practicing yoga for two hours daily. Additionally, we were required to do a specific and daily set of "tapas" practices as well. Unfortunately, I don't mean the traditional, small and delicious appetizer from Spain. In the context of yoga, "tapas" is about committing to your practice, staying focused, and embracing discomfort in order to purify your body and mind, which will lead to spiritual transformation. Practicing "tapas" involves a lot of discipline and inner strength. To me, it felt too rigid and forced. In the beginning, I was very enthusiastic, feeling excited to be part of the community, so I would put my needs in the background to fulfill the requirements. If we didn't do the practices, we were held accountable and reminded that we had to do them in order to be part of the community. I don't do well with rules that feel forced onto me, and those rules started to feel too rigid and dogmatic. I am a woman who loves being in the feminine flow and the long hours of meditation and hatha yoga practices didn't leave much room for my fluidity. I stopped committing to the daily practices if they didn't align with what I needed at the moment. I began to express how I was feeling and what I was missing, only to be met with resistance and backlash. I expressed that I don't condone being emotionally manipulated into guilt and shame for not being available for the community every moment I was there. Again, I was met with a lot of spiritual bypassing and gaslighting, blaming me while there was nothing wrong with the community. I started to go into another cycle of self-doubt, asking myself, "What is wrong with me?", "Why can I not fit in again?" I did not know at the time that I had unconsciously chosen a familiar environment. The pattern of self-doubt and the effects of being in a similar environment to the one I grew up in ran deep within me, and I questioned myself for around three months. I decided to open up to several people about my feelings and experiences. Some heard me and saw my perspective, which was valuable and validating. It showed me that I wasn't going crazy and that there really were issues within the community. However, there were others who did not seem to hear or understand me, and I had the sense that they instead felt attacked by my concerns about something they held precious. After almost ten months in the community, I couldn't stand it any longer and asked for some time off to gain some clarity. Apart from that, I was really craving some alone time, after constantly being surrounded by people.

I decided to leave for Spain and spend some time at our family vacation house, and it was exactly what I needed. I was beyond joyful spending time by myself, having my own room, bathroom, and kitchen to cook anything I wanted. I was in such bliss and only engaged in activities that brought me joy, without any connection to spirituality or spiritual practices. I allowed myself to have fun and rekindle the sense of joy I thought I had lost while in the community. Three weeks into my blissful holiday, I received a phone call asking me to shorten my vacation because they were short-staffed for the upcoming Silent Meditation Retreat. Every fiber in my being contracted, and a strong sense of resistance overcame me. I did not want to return and serve at a place that made me feel so horrible in my being. I was very hesitant and told them I would need time to think about it. In response, I faced emotional manipulation again, but this time, it felt more like they were trying to pamper me so I would agree to come back. Anyway, I insisted I needed a few days to consider it. Little did I know that two days later, the world would change forever due to the coronavirus. The center had to close its doors. I was so unbelievably happy that I didn't have to go back there.

For the longest time I was holding a grudge against this community. I blamed and shamed them for treating me so badly. While I still believe there were legitimate issues within the community and the leadership, I also have to recognize my role in this. I chose to be there and to engage in unhealthy behaviors too. The environment we grew up in shapes how we perceive the world and we tend to choose the same environments over and over again because this is also what our nervous system is attuned to. We do so until we become conscious of this unconscious pattern, and when we start to choose differently. That's when true transformation can begin. Today, I don't blame the community anymore as I can see the humanness behind their patterns, and I am aware that we are all just trying to do our best. We all have habits we might not even realize, and that's okay—we're always learning and growing in life.

Song: "I don't want to be" - Gavin DeGraw

EIGHT
A DEEPER INITIATION

ROUND THREE, back in Austria. This time, though, it was not entirely by my choice since corona forced the Yoga Center to close its doors. I found myself once again back in my apartment having no idea what to do or where to go in life as the world shut down. I must admit the first lockdown felt really good. Almost everything was closed and almost everyone was at home. It gave me permission to just be. To rest, spend lots of time in nature and integrate what had happened in the spiritual community. I felt almost in a state of bliss due to the most stunning spring and summer weather that year and no obligations to anyone. There were regulations in place allowing us to spend time outside in nature for mental health purposes, and that's what I did every day. During this first lockdown, the whole world slowed down and I experienced a deep sense of relaxation. There was no pressure from outside telling me to find a "normal" job or making me feel that my worth depended on being productive. I know many people had a different, possibly negative experience, but for me, it gave me the necessary time and space to rest and regain my strength. I resisted the urge to fill my time with activities labeled as "useful" by the collective, like working on myself, learning a new hobby or another skill. Instead, I honored my exhaustion from the intense past year at the yoga school and focused on doing what felt truly good to me. As the first lockdown came to an end, I began looking for a job. I wanted to avoid ending up in a toxic environment again like I had experienced in hospitality, so I decided to try something new and started working in an organic store. A big bonus was that a friend of mine was already working there and it was "lockdown safe," providing a stable income to pay for my new course that I enrolled in. Additionally, I made sure to surround myself with like-minded people who valued a healthy lifestyle, sustainable practices, and were somewhat open to spirituality. The positive aspect of the workplace was that I made a few close friends. I found myself in a family-run business with three sisters as my bosses. Little did I know that they would become such big mirrors, reflecting certain aspects and deeply ingrained patterns in my life that I wasn't ready to look at. Unfortunately, I ended up once more in a toxic work environment, with frequent screaming, belittling, and excessive control over the employees. I was back in Austria in another unhealthy work environment. WTF happened? I grew up with a high pain tolerance, so I endured this behavior for a few months. Thankfully, I got along well with my work colleagues, which made the whole situation bearable. Plus, the job provided enough money for me to survive and pursue the course I had decided to take, which was one of the best decisions of my life.

I started a training based on Somatic Experience and the divine feminine, led by one of my mentors, Blair Lindsey, who came magically into my life. Originally, I had signed up for a different course she was supposed to be a part of, but it got canceled due to corona. Out of curiosity, I was looking her up on Instagram and stumbled across this post, "Embodied Feminine Power Coaching Certification." I was immediately intrigued and arranged a call with her. We had a beautiful conversation and connected immediately, which also led her to accept me for the course. I didn't find much more information and actually had no idea what I was signing up for. I felt an instant pull to this course, even though it was a one-year commitment. The nervousness and fear I felt were familiar signs that this was a path worth exploring. The decision to join this program was one of the best decisions of my life. It became a profound initiation into embracing a more grounded and integrated body-based approach to my traumas and resulting patterns. I connected deeply with the frequency of the divine feminine, which has been guiding me ever since. This frequency transformed my life by inviting me to experience every aspect of life to its fullest expression. No matter how blissful or ugly the experience might be, there is no judgment, only this intelligent force of life moving through me, inviting me to be present with it and guiding me deeper into life. Besides that, the somatic practices transformed my life and reconnected me to my body in such a profound way like no other modality before. It brought me a deeper alignment and connection with the universe. This knowledge changed my whole outlook on life and spirituality. I learned techniques that helped me to release stored trauma in a healthier, softer and more integrated way. The combination of somatic work and reconnecting with the feminine deeply affected my body and nervous system, leading to a recalibration of my mind and innate feeling of worthiness. I became stronger and softer at the same time. Stronger in the sense of standing up more assertively for myself, my needs and desires, especially with family members, which was the most difficult part. Softer in the sense of reconnecting with my sensuality and sexuality through lots of body, pussy and womb work, but in a healthier and more integrated way than in my past. This aspect of myself was still within me, but after the abusive relationship, I had hidden it away again. The trauma was so overwhelming I did not even remember it until I started this training.

The program and the recalibration supported me in setting healthy boundaries in my surroundings, even though it was challenging at first due to the ingrained pattern of pleasing others and putting their needs before mine for almost 30 years. That's how I grew up, and what was known to me and my nervous system. The first few months into the training were very challenging. I barely had the energy to wake up, work and cook. I used to spend lots of time in nature as it seemed to be the only way to recharge my batteries. I also needed lots of sleep just to get through the day, which is normal when your nervous system starts to feel safe again after an extended period of being in a high alert state. Mine was in one due to the incredibly stressful and toxic work environment of the organic shop. Once you learn to regulate your nervous system to a healthy and balanced state, it is completely normal to move through a phase of increased fatigue and higher need for rest due to releasing stored stress, tension and trauma. I was incredibly grateful to have been in a guided coaching container during this time. Otherwise, I would probably have shamed myself for being "too lazy" or unable to "function normally".

Rest and relaxation are vital aspects of our overall well-being. Allowing our body to rest and recover can support the healing journey and promote a sense of balance and calmness within the nervous system. Impatience can hinder us on this journey because we haven't learned to purposefully rest and see it as an integral part of our lives. We may find this process too slow, but actually the slower we go and adapt to our own pace, the faster we transform and let go, as it happens in a more natural, integrated way with less resistance. Even though it was challenging for me at the beginning, I knew it was essential to give my body the rest it needed. Nature became, and is to this day, my sanctuary and life saver. Every day after work, I went for at least two hours into the forest to calm my nervous system, ground myself, and do some somatic breathwork to slowly release and integrate what happened during the day or week. Before that, it was really hard and almost too overwhelming for me and my system to engage in "normal" life again. Don't forget that on top of everything I was personally going through, we as a collective underwent a big traumatic experience as well, so life was just a lot for me at that time.

Despite all the healing, growing and learning I had undergone, the feeling that Austria was not my true home never left me. It felt more like a place that would keep me small, hinder my growth and prevent me from flourishing. I had spiraling thoughts, contemplating my situation for months:

What is wrong with me?

Why am I like this?

If I leave, would I be running away again, like I did when I was 18?

Is leaving this place really true to my heart?

Why does everyone feel so rooted here, but not me?

One thing I knew for sure was that the place I grew up in felt like a tiny fish tank that I had outgrown long ago. Especially now that I started working on myself, setting boundaries, and shedding the roles of the good girl, the people pleaser, and the easygoing chick without any needs, I experienced intense backlash and resistance from those closest to me. This led to many fights with friends and family due to me speaking up for myself and refusing to be pushed around anymore. We are all part of social systems, and changing my behavior meant the whole system needed to change. Whether these systems are family, groups of friends, associations, or a workplace, everyone plays a role that they subconsciously took over and/or has been assigned by others. My role was the agreeable, good girl and people pleaser who never stood up for herself and her needs or dared to speak up if I disliked something. I allowed myself to be pushed around because keeping the harmony was more important to me. Avoiding conflict was my coping strategy, being too afraid others would leave me all alone in the world. So, I started setting boundaries and speaking up for myself and what I wanted. I began to step out of my usual role, which scared the people closest to me. I stopped being available to be pushed around, controlled or manipulated. Taking responsibility and actually looking at my own pain, which I had been avoiding and projecting onto others through blaming and shaming, wasn't the most fun task. It brought up emotions like anger, frustration, and sadness that I had learned to avoid because they weren't considered "positive or nice." This caused so much resistance and backlash from those closest to me. They felt triggered and were invited to take a look at their own pain that activated their natural coping mechanisms. I felt they wanted me to slip back into my old role so everything would stay as is, and they wouldn't have to face the discomfort and pain they had been pushing away for so long. It was more comfortable for them to keep everything as it was. But, it meant staying true to my growth and healing journey, even if it meant challenging the present situation. Despite the big transformation I had undergone and challenging the status quo of my life, I was still struggling with immense self-doubt. Trusting myself was still a challenge, even though I had improved massively. I wondered if leaving my little village was the right choice or just my flight pattern being activated again. Actually, it was less contemplatingand more overthinking and driving myself crazy. It got to a point where I had just created too many distorted versions in my head, which left me feeling even more lost. I knew Austria was not my place, but I was the only one in my surroundings that felt that way, so naturally I assumed it was my fault for not fitting in. In all honesty, reflecting on it while writing, I avoided taking responsibility for myself and my life. It was easier to play the victim and blame my surroundings for not meeting my needs. Instead of recognizing some surroundings are simply not a long-term match. After nine months of overthinking, indulging in self-pity, successfully avoiding taking responsibility, and putting myself through more suffering than I wanted to, it was time to finally take action. I decided to pack up my life once again, release my apartment, let go of many material belongings and start over in Mexico. As soon as I decided to go to Mexico, I felt my whole body relax and open up after holding so much tension for a long time. Interestingly, once I finally took responsibility for my life and committed to this decision, synchronicities started to arise again. I would encounter "Mexico" everywhere.

I would be getting in my car, putting on a song from a random Spotify Playlist, and the song's name would be "Mexico" by "Mar Malade," and the first line of the song is, "Ohhh, I wanna go to Mexico."

Another day, another random song called "Traveler" by Luca Aprile came across my playlist and one line caught my attention, "You are taking off to Mexico…"

The most random one was definitely when the Austrian Embassy offered me a job in Mexico City. "Wait…What? How did they get my email address? How is this even possible?"

Things like this would happen to me constantly as soon as I was clear in my decision and started moving towards it. I love it when synchronicities like these happen because it shows me that I am in alignment with what I need to do next.

A DEEPER INITIATION

This time I stayed eight months in Mexico and really enjoyed it. I went for a quick visit to my beloved Ecuador and returned to Austria because I wanted to spend some time with friends and family for summer in Europe. I simply love the summer in Europe with its long days, lush green nature, hiking in beautiful mountains, many festivals and events and visits to friends all over Europe. The intention was to stay only for four months and then go back to Mexico, which didn't happen in the end. I never returned to Mexico. For some reason, it just didn't feel right.

Song: "Mexico" by Mar Malade

NINE
THE MELTDOWN REALIZATION

THE TRAINING on learning how to regulate my nervous system gave me so much insight into how I operate and what patterns are ruling my life. I see it in myself and my surroundings. It not only helped me to understand myself better, but to have more compassion for myself and realize that those are deep running patterns that I adopted in my childhood. Carl Jung said, "Until you make your unconscious conscious, it will direct your life and you will call it fate", which is so true. As long as I am unaware of my pattern, I can't change it and it will rule my life. I used to shame myself for not being how I was told to be, especially when I was about to embark on another journey. Every time I booked a flight, I got super excited and danced around my apartment because it was something to look forward to. Being far away always gave me a feeling of liberation and freedom from judgment for not fitting in with the "normal crowd" because I was outside my normal surroundings and society's expectations.

There is a whole range of emotions moving through me every time I decide it is time to embark on another adventure. Going on adventures for me means packing up my life and leaving for

THE MELTDOWN REALIZATION

several months. I prefer going for longer periods because I really like to immerse myself in the culture and get to know a country, wondering if I could possibly live there for a while. As I mentioned in the beginning, right now, I am in Australia. This is my 7th country and the 3rd continent that I am trying to make a living in, and it feels good at the moment. I am the most content I have been in a very long time. But coming here meant yet again packing up my life in Austria for the 7th time and leaving everything and everyone behind. But I was still full of doubts.

Something that has become very clear to me in the past month is that whenever I spend a few months in Austria, my self-doubts and self-shame intensify. My levels of doubt are at their highest right before I embark on another journey. That's also when I question my life the most. Questions like, "What am I doing with my life? What are we doing with our life? What do we want to do with our life?" become prominent and are valid. To answer those questions we have to become radically honest with ourselves and quit the justification of why we can't have certain desires. We have to confront our fears, doubts, and insecurities head-on. This is not always an easy process, I know. It is equally essential that we don't let ourselves be held down by others, simply for not fitting into the picture they have painted. Here is a good example: once I got into a huge fight with a family member, where I was being yelled at with hurtful words and statements. According to her, I was being stupid and naive and wouldn't figure out my life. She accused me of acting like a little, dumb teenager, not taking responsibility for my life and just running after what I wanted. I was 30 years old at that time and took more responsibility for my life than this particular family member liked, because I was willing to go in another direction and actually follow what felt true to my heart. But this didn't fit into her picture of me, which probably scared her. She wanted me to stay in Austria and be "normal" like everyone else.

My breaking out could also have been a mirror for her. She might have once had this dream too, but never acted on it and I reminded her of a missed opportunity. Nevertheless, this encounter hurt me deeply, as I was highly insecure then. But I am glad I didn't let myself be held back by that.

The fourth and last time I spent in Austria was from July 2022 until March 2023. Nine months. That time felt like one of the hardest of my life. I found myself once again very lost and stuck without any idea of what to do with my life. I am in a place that does not feel like home, but I grew up here, so everything was known. It was known to my being and nervous system. It seemed easy to just stay here. Where else would I go? That is often the thing; just because it is known to you and your nervous system and is seemingly the easier choice, it might not necessarily be the healthiest choice. This is because the job of our nervous system is to ensure our survival and protect us from any potential danger. Anything new and unknown falls into the category of a potential threat, which is why we very much feel resistance against change. This can happen consciously or unconsciously. That is the reason we unconsciously choose the same environments, for example, the one we grew up in. It is known to our being and nervous system and seems to be a "safer choice," even though it might not be. To our nervous system, the unknown represents potential danger because it is unpredictable. That's when somatic work can be very valuable, because many of these unconscious choices and protection mechanisms are outdated. It is on us to become aware of them and rewire our nervous system for healthier choices.

Even though I learned this a few years ago and knew it, I still chose to stay longer in Austria, because it was known to me and my system and because going back to Mexico didn't feel right at the time and I had no idea where else to go. Not realizing that led to the biggest meltdown ever. I cried for a month straight. I

THE MELTDOWN REALIZATION

was completely overwhelmed with everything and my nervous system went into complete shutdown and freeze mode. Freeze mode is the third survival strategy of the nervous system, when fight or flight mode isn't feasible. The challenge for me being in the freeze response is that it only increased my thoughts, doubts and shame about myself. The state of our nervous system determines our thoughts, not the mind as we are often told. If you change the state of your nervous system and start to heal and come back to a natural balance between the sympathetic and parasympathetic, it will change how you think.

So here I found myself once again feeling very lost, lonely and stuck, but most of all, I felt stupid and ashamed, which only increased the stress on my nervous system and made me shut down even more and go deeper into the freeze response. I was so ashamed that I was here again, feeling the same way I felt almost a year ago. On top of that, it wasn't the first time, it was the fourth time, the fourth loop that I put myself in. Didn't I learn the lesson from the last time? Do I really have to put myself again through this situation? Additionally, I faced challenges with the relationship between my mother and me. It seems that with age, her fears grew bigger, especially around feeling safe. This meant she wanted to have her loved ones close to maintain a sense of control in her life. This sense of not being safe was obviously being triggered by my constant traveling around the world, which is very unsafe in her eyes. The difficulty for me here is that whenever I am back in Austria, she becomes very protective and clingy, trying to ensure my well-being and maintain a close connection with me. The challenging part for me here is that even though it is well intended, she often ignores my boundaries and refuses to accept that I am a grown woman, having my own life. But the childhood pattern of me having to always be available to her needs was still running deep through me, so me setting boundaries with her was something new for both of us. I was not used to doing that with her, so standing up to her was the most difficult thing for me. Whenever I would do that, knowing that this was the best thing for my well-being, I would feel so much guilt due to my nervous system being attuned to the opposite. Only with lots of self-regulation and simply learning to be with those uncomfortable feelings and knowing that they are part of the process of rewiring my nervous system, was I able to handle the situations. Since she was also not used to me setting boundaries, she would very often overstep them, which led to me crumbling and giving in many times, creating an unhealthy dance between us. Me trying to set boundaries, but still lacking the assertiveness and strength to hold them up.

Another aspect that gave me strength and support during these challenging times of redirecting my relationship with my mother and my family was learning about codependent relationships, which brought so much clarity to me. I began to see my role in it and the victimhood that I kept myself in. I completely blamed my mother for everything instead of taking ownership of my role and my life. I have always thought of myself as quite an independent woman, since I left home at 18 years old to live somewhere completely new, and continued to do so throughout the last 16 years. I am an independent woman in many aspects of my life, but learning about codependency made me realize that in many aspects I was also not as independent as I would have liked, which was a painful awakening. The clarity I have gained through seeing the subtle behaviors I still engage in that would keep me in this codependent relationship helped me to slowly but consciously untangle myself and truly separate myself from my parents to embody my true independence. I have to confess that it is not easy to admit in this book that in my 30s I was still dependent on my parents in many ways. Honestly, who wants to admit something like that? In a culture that values

THE MELTDOWN REALIZATION

independence so much, being still somewhat dependent on your parents at that age is almost seen as shameful and childish.

However, at a certain point, challenging the status quo of the relationship with my mother had become even more overwhelming to my already shut-down nervous system, and I had the deep need to create some distance and space for me to just be. As I simply didn't have the energy to go to another country and start over again by myself, another family member offered to let me stay in an empty 1-bedroom apartment of hers, which I thankfully accepted. I was grateful to have a little time and space away from the daily family drama I put myself in by staying in my hometown. Unfortunately, little did I know that I was walking right into the next challenging situation.

I have noticed that when I am unstable in my body, I feel more open to being influenced by the opinions of others, especially on how to live my life. I lacked stability within myself and, as a result, the necessary assertiveness needed to stand up for myself and my different viewpoint on life. Instead of simply accepting that both viewpoints can coexist, I wasted energy trying to justify myself. Your surroundings greatly affect you and can influence your opinion and viewpoint. Since I was surrounded mostly by people who were living how society intended it for us, it started to rub off on me and that's where the biggest self-doubts around my life started to sneak in.

As unstable as I was then, whenever I talked to the family member who let me stay in her space, I would find myself constantly arguing and trying to explain my different points of view. She wouldn't listen and drowned me in counter arguments on why my way of living was not good and at my age no longer acceptable. As I mentioned in the beginning, in your 30s, you should have figured life out by now, whatever that means, and for me, not "being there" was often accompanied by shame. The arguments I tried to escape with my mother started coming back around with this family member, which was mostly that it was time for me to settle down in Austria or somewhere else and let go of my vagabond lifestyle. I tried to explain and justify myself to her, but it seemed like hitting a concrete wall. Reflecting on it, I realized that I was probably justifying more to myself than to her due to feeling so insecure about my way of living. Apart from that, deep down, my inner child just wanted to be accepted for who I was and wanted approval from my family to do things differently. I just wanted to hear and feel, "You are doing a good job finding your own way." or "I support you." I know my family supports me, but it is one thing to kind of know and another to actually hear it.

Having the same arguments with this particular family member I had with my mother took so much effort and energy that it led to an even deeper freeze response. I would cry for no reason, I didn't have any energy, and I slept a lot. I barely had energy for the basic things; work, cook, maybe meet up with some friends, but that's it. I hit rock bottom hard, but this time it truly clicked for me that I just couldn't live in Austria anymore. I have always had this feeling, which was the main reason for me leaving so many times and trying to live in so many different countries, but this time it really landed in my body. I could feel it in every fiber of my being; this was simply a different knowing. It felt deeper, more rooted, more true, than when it was just a thought. I realized how much unnecessary suffering I put myself through all those times by immersing myself in a world that doesn't align with me and my values, and just makes me feel miserable every time I spend too much time in Austria. That was when I finally accepted that I didn't want to live as society expects me to, and that was absolutely ok. I stopped blaming and resenting society for what it was and just accepted that I was not compatible with that way of living, which brought immense relief to my body. I

THE MELTDOWN REALIZATION

had already booked my flight to Australia, and my goal was to survive as comfortably as possible in the upcoming months until my departure date. From that moment on, I tried to engage more in self-regulation tools and learned more about the freeze response that I was in. Gentle activities are better to help you move out of a freeze response than high-intense ones, as they could overwhelm your system, and result in further shutdown. Soft and gentle activities that are stimulating enough, but not too much, are key here. Moving at a slow and integrated pace that allows you to increase the capacity of the nervous system is necessary to hold uncomfortable emotions. This creates a connection with your body by asking what it wants, needs and is key in moving through different trauma responses. That meant taking my time and cooking nourishing food for myself, going into nature for walks and trying to engage all the senses. Physical touch through loved ones, massages and self-caressing help the body to feel safe again and open up. Being in a freeze response also means that you "froze" certain emotions you had before you went into shutdown, so moving out of this response can resurface those emotions. That's why working on feeling safe and increasing your capacity to hold those emotions is vital. We have to be aware that this could make us feel worse before we feel better.

Feeling alone, not really seen or understood, was a big part of my experience in Austria. I have sweet friends I have known for many years that I trust and open up to about what is happening inside me. Despite that, I only felt seen and understood to a certain extent, simply because most of them live very different lifestyles, which made me question if it is even possible for them to truly understand me when they have never been in my shoes. I love them and trust them with my inner world, yet sometimes I feel more seen by people I meet during my travels than by those who have known me for decades. Simply because the people I meet on the road have similar stories to mine, leaving their homes because they don't want to go down the paved way of society. When I was growing up, I sometimes felt there was no space for me, for being different in a world that tells us to conform to be a valuable member of this community/society. Traveling and meeting so many different people from all over the world, yet with similar intentions like mine, was a truly eye-opening experience and a big relief to my system. It was confirmation that I am not the crazy one or the outsider I have felt like my entire life. There are many more people out there than I ever imagined feeling the same way. I started not to feel so lonely and lost anymore. I felt truly seen and understood.

Whenever I am not surrounded by friends or other people with similar points of view on life, I start to look for very specific podcasts and I listen to them constantly to keep myself from going crazy. It helps to remind me that I am not alone with this viewpoint in the world. Obviously, it can't substitute having like-minded people around you, but it is a good bridge until you find yourself with those people again.

Song: "What would I know" - Jeremy Loops

TEN
TRUST AND MAGIC WILL HAPPEN

LEARNING to trust the process was and is an essential part of moving through life. In my experience, "trusting the process" can either be one of the hardest or easiest things to do, depending on where you are and how you feel at the moment. It is definitely easier being here in Australia, where so many magical things started happening, and with me receiving so much. When I was back in Austria amidst my transformation and struggle, I was unclear and desperate about the next steps in my life. It was definitely harder, mostly due to me refusing to accept what was actually happening. I realized I needed to be where I was back then. I vividly remember wanting this phase to be over as soon as possible. I was so done with repeating the same old pattern. I asked the universe for signs and next steps and kept receiving the message: "It is not time yet." This triggered my impatience, making it harder to trust and simply be present. One day, while talking to my friend Emilia in Australia, I told her about my idea of visiting her, but the flights were too expensive. Without hesitation, and more out of curiosity, she went online, started looking for flights and promptly found a flight for only €450. That's when I couldn't hesitate and booked it right away. The deal was simply too good to let it pass. There were still four months until my departure date, and though I was super excited and danced around my apartment after booking, I also had moments of doubt during that time. The decision was made and whenever I was in doubt the universe would send me a clear sign. One of my favorite examples of receiving clear signs was at my friend Rachel's birthday/Christmas party. She invited us to bring presents we owned that held meaning for us, but we were willing to let go. I didn't initially realize that we would also do a Secret Santa exchange with her other friends who were attending the party. There were seven ladies in total and we all hadn't met before. Yet when it came to exchanging gifts, something amazing happened, every single one of us received the perfect gift. I received a tiny Buddha statue. I loved it and had such a big smile when I opened it! What made this so special for me was that I wished for a tiny travel Buddha statue about two years prior to that when I first saw it in my friend Emilia's home, right before she moved back to Australia. The same friend I was about to visit in Australia. There couldn't have been a clearer sign that I was on the right path.

Looking back at my time in Austria now, I was always being guided and protected by the universe, leading me towards what was best for me at that moment. One of the most valuable lessons I learned was learning to work with the nervous system and its profound impact on our lives. Through my experiences, I gained insights I can now share with others so they can live to the fullest. Had I not gone through the intense phases in Austria, I probably wouldn't feel so firm and stable in my being now. I have a clearer understanding of what I want in life. It shaped me into the person I am today, for which I am grateful.

During my process of feeling immensely unstable, pushed around and walked over, which I let happen due to my lack of boundaries, I came to realize that I had surrounded myself with the wrong people for too long, even if those people were near and dear to me. It took hitting rock bottom four times before I finally understood the importance of accepting that life in Austria, with its values and environment, was not aligned with who I am.

Since arriving in Australia, I have noticed how things are starting to fall into place for me now, this book being one example. The idea of writing a book has been lingering in the back of my head for a few years now, but I never felt courageous enough to follow up on this desire. Letting myself be held back by my fear of being seen and thoughts like, "Who would want to read this?" However, on my birthday in early February of this year, I had the idea for this book and boom, two days later, a newsletter from my book coach and publisher that I have been following on Instagram for about two years now landed in my inbox. It announced a five-day book-writing bootcamp. Without much hesitation, I decided to take part in the bootcamp, even while traveling to different countries. I knew it was time to take a leap, and made it happen. As she announced her new group coaching program, a familiar mix of feeling equally nervous and excited came up, signaling I was on the right path.

As I arrived in Australia, I wanted some time to slowly unwind and set myself up for the upcoming trip around the country. I brought only clothes and personal items in my backpack, so I needed to start from scratch by buying a car and all the camping gear necessary for living on the road. I gradually adapted to this completely new country I had never been to before, with its unique accent and slang that I found challenging to understand. It took a while to adapt to driving on the left side (for me, that's the wrong side) of the road. By the time the course started, I was completely set up in a beautiful campsite at the Sunshine Coast, ready to dive deep into this transformational process. Throughout the process of writing this book, I continued to receive so many signs along the way, especially in times of doubt. I have met an author at every place I stayed during this writing process. I can't recall meeting an actual book author before, but within six weeks and three different places, I have met three different persons who have either published a book or are about to. That is the universe's way of confirming that I am on the right path.

Over the years, I've developed the habit of asking for a sign whenever I'm in doubt and the universe always delivers! The key is to have unwavering trust that the sign will come. When I was living in Mexico I wanted to go to Ecuador, since I was already on the same side of the globe. Unfortunately, I couldn't enter the country at first due to its restrictive Corona regulations. I tried to let go of the idea. But a few months later, I woke up one morning with the sudden urge to check for the entry regulations in Ecuador again to see if anything had changed. To my surprise, they had changed and I was allowed to enter. Excited and happy about that, I checked for flights and saw they were reasonably priced. I asked the universe for a sign if it would be in my highest alignment to leave for Ecuador. If so, please send me the number 555. I went to bed, woke up, and had the urge to look for flights again and I stumbled upon a flight with its departure time at 15:55. There it was, my confirmation! I immediately booked a flight and left about two weeks later, knowing deep down that this was the path meant for me, even though my mind gave me a hard time. I questioned my decision to leave Mexico again after only six months and leaving my intentions to create a home base there. In moments of doubt, the universe responded with repetitive signs, presenting the number 555 everywhere – on number plates, social media, prices, and even the time. I am grateful that I followed by flying to Ecuador. Only a few weeks later, the little village of Mazunte, which I had intended to make my home, was struck by hurricane Agatha and nearly destroyed. The experience left me in awe, realizing that I had been protected and guided by the universe, sparing me from living through such an intense experience.

As I was flying over Ecuador, I immediately had the feeling of coming back home even after not being there for five years. I had the urge to return, and it was as if I had left a part of myself behind in Ecuador. I always looked back in nostalgia. As if the universe was orchestrating again, the next sign of divine alignment was when the apartment next to a dear friend of mine suddenly became available. A family was meant to move in there, but they couldn't move to Ecuador for some reason, leaving the apartment open for me. I loved being back in Ecuador, reminiscing on old memories, reconnecting with old friends and making new ones. I wanted to stay longer, but I had already organized my return flight to Europe, departing from Cancun in Mexico. After the cold climate in Quito, I wanted to spend an additional two weeks in the warmth of Mexico and I secured a house-sit for the two weeks before my return. Initially, I thought it was the perfect plan! Then, I wanted to extend my stay in Ecuador, as I was having such a good time. Trusting the process, I once again asked for guidance from the universe, "Is it in my highest alignment to go to Mexico?" This time, I didn't ask for a number but a sign. My intuition and gut feeling were leaning towards Mexico, even though I initially resisted. But the word "Merida," which was the name of the city I had arranged the house-sit for, kept appearing. I trusted it was in my highest alignment, even though my ego resisted. Once again, I am grateful I trusted my intuition. Just two days before my departure from Ecuador, the indigenous people began protesting against the economic policies of the president. They marched from various regions towards Quito, resulting in the streets being closed down so no one would be able to enter or leave the city. The city went into a state of emergency for almost the entire two weeks I spent in Merida. Again, I was protected and guided by the universe. If I had stayed, I would have been in a city that was shut down, and I could not have left my apartment the entire time.

Those are only a few examples of what can happen if we trust ourselves, our intuition and the universe. The key, in my experience, is to clearly ask for signs, let go, and then trust that the answers will come. I've found that asking for clear and specific signs helps, especially in the beginning when I might not always receive or recognize them right away. But as we open ourselves to the guidance of the universe, it becomes easier to see the signs and follow the path that is meant for us. Repeating number patterns has become my love language with the universe. Throughout the day, I notice certain numbers appearing over and over again. Depending on what I need to focus on, these number patterns can vary, and over time, I've deciphered their message and meaning for myself.

After practicing this for a few years, I have started to notice other signs too. I will receive messages in songs, billboards, phrases that stick out to me, or even material signs like the little travel Buddha. Today, I've also developed a strong sense in my body. When something's right for me, I feel an open, expansive space in my chest. When it's not, I feel a contraction. Again, the key to this is to trust oneself without doubting, questioning, or overthinking. Especially in the beginning, it requires much more trust and patience, which won't always be there. But that is ok, just keep practicing. If a sign is not clear enough, ask for a clearer sign until you get it, don't start looking or searching for the signs. When I was too impatient and started looking for signs, like numbers I asked for, I wouldn't see them. But the minute I let go and be like, "fuck it, it will come when it will come," I see it. This very often makes me smile and reminds me that I sometimes prolong my waiting period by being impatient and actively searching for it instead of just trusting that they will arrive at their perfect timing. That's when true magic will start happening and the more you trust it, the more you will start seeing the evidence. Since I arrived in Australia, so much magic has happened to me. I have been receiving so much love, help and acts of kindness in so many different forms from strangers like never before. I am not used to that, but I see it as an invitation to learn to simply receive and be grateful. The more I receive, the more I want to give and reciprocate. It might not be to the same person, but that does not matter. I feel like it is a cycle of receiving and offering, and it is about the energy that is reciprocated.

Song: "Don't you worry" - Black Eyed Peas

ELEVEN
LIFE IS TOO SHORT NOT TO LIVE ACCORDING TO YOUR TERMS

AFTER ALL THE struggle and transformation I have gone through in the past 16 years of trying to break free, I realize that living a life that feels worthy of living to YOU is all that matters! Living a life in alignment with what you desire and believe is true to your heart. No matter what anyone else says. I felt this lack of belonging in so many different groups throughout my life because I was trying to force-fit myself into environments that didn't truly align with me. Hence, there was always a feeling of lack that I had been desperately trying to fill. By doing so, I abandoned parts of myself, by hiding them or putting masks on, which only created a bigger void within myself. I have been creating a life that feels true to me and traveling the world, living in many different countries, creating my own business and living according to my timeline has been a big part of that. In creating my own path, I have found a profound sense of belonging in itself, because I finally understood that the more authentic I am, the freer I feel. As we have established in this book, a sense of true, embodied freedom is one of the most important values in my life. At first, I thought true freedom came from breaking free from the societal path of living. Even though doing that did bring me a certain extent of freedom, it wasn't fully embodied. True, embodied freedom can come only from within, when we fully embrace and express our most authentic and truest self, shedding all the layers and masks we put on due to societal expectations or as a defense mechanism. It arises when we let go of the self-limiting beliefs and fears holding us back, opening up our hearts, becoming more vulnerable and inviting growth and self-discovery through that. True freedom arises as a state of being, when we truly connect with our own deepest values and desires that are true to us. True freedom invokes feelings like liberation, empowerment, aliveness, vibrancy, contentment and joy in every fiber of our being. It gives us the strength to live fully and unapologetically. This is a constant process of shedding what no longer serves us and embracing what is true to us, inviting us deeper and deeper into our most authentic selves. Don't get me wrong; it is not an easy and certainly not a linear process. I stopped counting the times I wanted to give up, but I am glad I never did because letting go of every layer is so damn worth it. There are still so many limiting beliefs and fears in my being and I think they will never end. Whenever I let go of one layer, there is an invitation into another, deeper layer. But on the other side to every limiting belief, there is an invitation to go into another, deeper layer of my own truth. I have tried to outrun uncomfortable feelings by traveling far and long and chasing the concept of freedom. Needless to say, those feelings always caught up with me until I stopped running, turned around and truly faced them. I have tried to outrun, or in my case, "out travel" the emotion of feeling stuck as much as I could. Even here in Australia, this pattern tried to sneak back in. After the first excitement and newness of being in a new country wears off, this feeling of being stuck tries to come back in, and I resent it. The more I resented it, the louder and stronger it became until I realized that this is just a part of life, especially when you create your own path and don't know the next steps. As soon as I accepted that this was a part of my life, I relaxed. That's when clarity about my next step came in on how to move away from this feeling. I am writing this book while living on the road from different campsites. My initial intention was to find one spot I felt comfortable in, set myself up and stay there for the entire writing process. Well, that didn't happen. I changed my location three times, because of this feeling of being stuck, which I also often relate to monotony. This time, however, I recognized it, accepted it, and took responsibility for being the true creator of my life by taking action to change that. While it is important to face our feelings and not avoid or flee from them, it's equally important to realize when it's time to take action toward change. Don't forget to celebrate yourself for recognizing a common pattern and taking action toward it. I reduced my time of realization of feeling stuck from nine months to two weeks. If that is not one hell of an improvement and worth celebrating, I don't know what is! As I said in the beginning, celebrating and acknowledging yourself for every step, no matter how small or big, towards the life you desire is important.

It is never too late to start changing your life. You are not too old, young, inexperienced or any other limiting belief you keep telling yourself. It is your life and the time is now! You can start changing it by taking baby steps so it feels less daunting. Sometimes, there will be a sense of impatience coming in and you'll already want to be somewhere else without really going through the process of getting there. I have been there and know this feeling too well. I have realized that you should try to enjoy the process of living life according to your terms, because it will never be like this again. Every moment is transient. My wish for you is that something in these pages will inspire you to reconnect to your own drumbeat. It is there, I promise you, but it might just be hiding somewhere deep down in your being. I

LIFE IS TOO SHORT NOT TO LIVE ACCORDING TO YOUR TE...

know your drumbeat is different too, or you would not be holding this book in your hands right now. Being different is your greatest asset and will impact and invite the people in your surroundings to reconnect to their drumbeat as well. You are not alone in this! I see you!

Song: "Unstoppable" - Sia

ACKNOWLEDGMENTS

Writing a book is undoubtedly a transformational journey in itself. The idea of writing this book had been lingering in the back of my mind for several years, but I never quite felt ready to share my story. The idea sparked from a sentence a friend said to me during my 2023 birthday getaway: 'Despite all the challenges and resistance you faced, you did it anyway, and that's something you can be proud of!' This idea was born from a mix of excitement and nervousness.

Two days later, an invitation to a 5-day bootcamp writing workshop from my publisher, Sandra, landed in my inbox. I knew this wasn't a coincidence. After the bootcamp, I couldn't let the opportunity to join her group program pass by, even though it scared me. And now, here we are. I am grateful to Sandra for her genuine, gentle, flexible guidance in helping me find my voice and my story. Thank you, Sandra, for taking me on this transformational journey and for your continuous support and empowerment throughout the entire process. I'd also like to express my gratitude to her wonderful team: Nadia, for her copy editing expertise, and Nicolette, for her technical and book formatting skills.

To my friends — Linda, Isabel, Isidor, Robin and Sheela — who supported me from afar. Thank you for being there during my low moments when tough memories resurfaced. Thank you for providing feedback and helping me brainstorm ideas. Thank you for your pep talks and for reminding me, "You've got this! I believe in you!" when I needed to hear it.

To Sam, thank you for your presence and for being there during my low moments, for listening, providing feedback, and nurturing me on all levels—physically, emotionally, mentally, and spiritually. Our genuine, open, honest, and vulnerable conversations have inspired and sparked many ideas in this book.

To Dave and your incredible skills! Thank you for working with me on various levels to help me remain calm and centered in my being while writing this book.

To the many people I met while traveling in Australia who have inspired me through their presence, conversations, kindness, generosity, openness, vulnerability, and the space they held for me, thank you.

And last but not least, to my family, who always had my back and helped me realize the dream of writing a book

THANK YOU

To all my dear readers: Thank you for taking the time and reading my book.

As you follow your own drumbeat towards more aliveness and vibrancy in your life, connect with Claudia and share your stories. Let's inspire each other and support each other. We are not alone in this.

Instagram: https://www.instagram.com/claudiastoeckler/
Facebook: https://www.facebook.com/claudia.stoeckler
Website: www.claudiastoeckler.com

Email me for the complete Spotify playlist, with all the songs mentioned in the book and a little surprise!

stoeckler.claudia@gmail.com

ABOUT THE AUTHOR

Claudia Stöckler is a Somatic and Embodiment Coach helping women in reconnecting to their own drumbeat and rediscovering what truly makes them feel alive.From a young age, she realized that her own rhythm was different. Although born and raised in the beautiful Austrian Alps, her heart was set on exploring the world. She has lived in seven different countries on three different continents, following her own drumbeat rather than conforming to societal expectations. Along this journey, she faced numerous challenges, setbacks, and occasional returns to patterns she tried to outrun or in her case "outtravel." Only to realize her true freedom comes from within.

Each country offered a distinct experience and an invitation to uncover a new aspect of her true self. When she found the teaching of Somatic Experience combined with the energies of the divine feminine things started to profoundly shift and change in her life. Claudia has found deep relief and insight into her own traumas, behaviors and patterns that have been unconsciously running her life and holding her back form the truly magical and vibrant life she wanted to live.

Today, she shares the knowledge and experiences she has gathered over the years through private mentorships with other women. She guides women back into their bodies to feel safe, sovereign and vibrant. Her approach is slow, integrated and trauma-informed integrative, and trauma-informed, incorporating various embodiment techniques and somatic, erotic movement practices. Claudia brings a gentle and nurturing energy to her work, assisting her clients in transforming their pain into pleasure.

Connect with Claudia on Instagram: https://www.instagram.com/claudiastoeckler/

www.ingramcontent.com/pod-product-compliance
Lightning Source LLC
Chambersburg PA
CBHW022120040426
42450CB00006B/784